Learning through talking 11–16

SCHOOLS COUNCIL WORKING PAPER 64

Learning through talking 11–16

the report of the Schools Council/
Avon Education Authority
Language Development Project
based at Weston Teachers' Centre (1975–77)

Evans/Methuen Educational

*First published 1979 for the Schools Council
160 Great Portland Street London W1N 6LL
by Evans Brothers Limited
Montague House, Russell Square, London WC1B 5BX
and Methuen Educational
11 New Fetter Lane, London EC4P 4EE*

© *Schools Council Publications 1979*

*Printed in Great Britain by
Richard Clay (The Chaucer Press) Ltd
Bungay, Suffolk*

British Library Cataloguing in Publication Data

Schools Council/Avon Education Authority Language
Development Project.
Learning through talking 11–16. – (Schools Council.
Working papers; 64 ISSN 0533–1668).
1. Learning 2. Oral communication – Great Britain
3. Communication in education – Great Britain
I. Title II. Series
370.15′2   LB1060
ISBN 0 423 50710 9

Contents

Acknowledgements

The Schools Council and the publishers are grateful to Editions Gallimard, Paris (1949) for permission to use the poem 'Page d'écriture' ['Exercise Book'] from *Paroles* by Jacques Prévert and to The Bodley Head for the use of the Paul Dehn translation of this poem from *For Love and Money* (1956); to the Controller of Her Majesty's Stationery Office for the use of extracts from *A Language for Life* [The Bullock Report], (HMSO, 1975); and to Cambridge University Press for the use of two graphs in Chapter V from *The School Mathematics Project: Book D* (1969).

Preface

Some teachers still set pupils the task of writing out lines such as 'I must not talk in class' as a punishment for talking during a lesson. The note of dissent to the Bullock Report, *A Language for Life* (HMSO, 1975) clearly supports the attitude that talking in class is inappropriate:

> It is doubtful if children's talk in school does much to improve their knowledge, for free discussion as a learning procedure at any age is notoriously unproductive.

However, since children communicate considerably more frequently through talking than by means of writing, it seems likely that they can gain something from being allowed to talk in class. Child psychologists know that small children cannot learn effectively unless they talk. It surely follows that the education of secondary-school children should include an element of 'learning through talking'. Douglas Barnes in *From Communication to Curriculum* (Penguin Books, 1976) writes:

> Pupils' talk is important in that it is a major means by which learners explore the relationship between what they already know and new observations and interpretations which they meet.

The poem 'Exercise Book' by Jacques Prévert expresses this idea in imagery: it does not suggest that learning tables is irrelevant, nor that talking (or singing) is preferable; rather that there is a world of experience beyond the classroom which, if some way were found of dissolving the classroom walls, could add the wide world of the child's experience and imaginative vision to the restricted domain of the classroom:

> Two and two are four
> Four and four are eight
> eight and eight are sixteen . . .

Again! says the teacher
Two and two are four
four and four are eight
eight and eight are sixteen.
But look! the lyre-bird flying past
the child sees it
the child hears it
the child calls out to it
Save me
play with me
bird!
Then the bird comes down
and plays with the child.
Two and two are four . . .
Again! says the teacher
And the child plays
and the bird plays with him . . .
Four and four are eight
eight and eight are sixteen
and what are sixteen and sixteen?
Nothing
least of all thirty-two
however you look at it
and off they go.
And the child has hidden the bird
in his desk
and the whole class
hears him singing
the whole class
hears the music
and eight and eight in their turn
off they go
and four and four and two and two
off they go too and
one and one are neither one nor two
but one by one away they go.
And the lyre-bird plays
and the child sings
and the teacher yells:
When you've finished mucking around!
But everyone else
is listening to the music
and the classroom walls

come tumbling quietly down.
And the window-panes are sand again
the ink is water
the desks are trees
the chalk is a cliff
and the quill pen is again a bird.

There is much in a child's experience which can never enter the classroom if the child is made to sit still and listen, or to do exercises or to read and write, nearly all the time silently. When children are allowed to talk they gain the opportunity to put something of themselves into their learning, and to learn by exploring their own experience and putting it against the 'new observations and interpretations which they meet' in school. If they are discouraged from talking their learning may remain rote learning; if they are allowed to talk they may well disturb the peace of the classroom, but they may also discover for themselves the relevance of what might otherwise remain rote learning.

In the experience of those of us involved in the Schools Council/Avon Education Authority Language Development Project, learning through talking is an important and to some extent neglected element in the whole educational process. We believe that talk can improve children's knowledge by helping them make that knowledge their own, and we hope that *Learning through Talking 11–16* will enable teachers to come some way to meet the child and his lyre-bird.

GEOFFREY EGGINS
Project Director

Introduction

This book is the culmination of many years' work. That work began as one teacher's study of the place of English in the third year of the secondary school and became a group study of talk in the first to fifth years of the secondary school. The work was funded from 1975 to 1977 jointly by the Schools Council and the Avon Education Authority as a local curriculum development project, and was based at the teachers' centre at Westcliff in Weston-super-Mare.

In 1975, at the time of its funding, the project involved teachers from the eight comprehensive schools in Woodspring, that part of Avon served by the Weston Teachers' Centre. The project director was head of English at one of those schools, on secondment for two days a week over two years. Those involved in the project are listed at the end of the book.

Extent of the project's work
Although the work began as a study of the spoken language of third-year pupils it naturally extended its scope to include the first and second years and the fourth and fifth years as interest was shown in those earlier years and as third-year pupils moved up the school. Project members' schools and classroom experiences were as varied as one might reasonably expect in a predominantly middle-class area, but the teachers' centre (where the project had an office, a part-time secretary and recourse to the services of a technician) provided a unifying and vivifying force emanating from small-group meetings, large-group meetings and conferences. Thus the teachers' centre became a power-house into which ideas and experiences came in the form of tapes and tape-transcripts and records of lessons for discussion by project members and their colleagues, visitors from other schools and people from training colleges and universities. From the teachers' centre flowed ideas and enthusiasm arising from the fresh perceptions of classroom activity which those discussions generated. Thus, and further united by the project director's constant visits to schools, the group developed a dynamic which is represented severally by the individual contributions to

this book, but totally by the whole book. The contributions of individuals emanate necessarily and organically from their membership of the project as a whole.

At the time when official funding started in 1975, project members shared a general enthusiasm for and interest in the use of talk in their lessons which arose from the fact that they were committed English teachers and had been working together already for some time. At that stage, however, their enthusiasm was largely uneducated in that they tended to act by intuition rather than from an explicit awareness of how they could control and monitor talk in their classrooms and identify those features of pupil talk which they and other teachers might regard as unique and valuable. They shared with many other teachers a certain lack of confidence in the use of talk in the classroom, and an implicit suspicion about its ultimate value.

A personal view of the place of talk in teaching
Early in the history of the project each project member was asked to write down thoughts about his involvement in the project. One of those contributions is quoted below. It indicates how the contributing teachers approached the work with a mixture of uncertainty generated by the suspicions of fellow teachers, and enthusiasm engendered by their own intuitive realization of the value of talk in the classroom:

> 'Be quiet that boy at the back there. Will you please get on with your work and stop talking.' Surely there can be few adults to whom these words do not have a familiar ring.

> Certainly, they conjure up in my mind an almost tangible memory of the classroom; hours spent toiling over a grubby exercise book, the pungent aroma of boys' sweaty bodies, the air thick with chalk dust and the sonorous drone of the teacher's voice. Perhaps this is one reason why I became interested in the place of oral English in the syllabus, and I am sure that the fact that I grew up with the fixed belief that talking in school was the very antithesis of what education was all about explains why, even now, I am more at home when setting my thoughts down on paper, than when I am endeavouring to expound those same thoughts to an assemblage of critical and often sceptical colleagues.

> Of course, it is all different now. In these enlightened times, children are not only allowed to have opinions but are also allowed, and even encouraged, to express them; or so it is generally assumed. Yet, from my experience from the other side of the educational fence, I am not at all sure that this is the case. While there are few teachers who would go so far as to deny the importance

of the acquisition of oral as well as literary skills, there are several inhibiting factors which militate against the lesson designed to encourage talking rather than writing.

The first of these, as I have already implied, is that many teachers are influenced as much by their own experiences as pupils as they are by suggestions which were made during their professional training. They therefore feel that perhaps their lessons should follow the well-worn paths with which they are themselves familiar.

Secondly, it is irrefutable that a situation in which a class is talking is also a situation in which the teacher has little apparent control. It is very easy for the teacher to feel superfluous, and therefore to feel that he is 'not doing his job'. This brings me to the third inhibiting factor – noise. Most teachers are sensitive about their professional efficiency, and a noisy classroom tends to indicate inefficiency. We are all familiar with the philosophy which states that quiet is synonymous with learning and noise is synonymous with anarchy.

Nor is the problem of noise confined merely to one's own classroom; the design of many of our schools is far from helpful. It is one thing to allow an 'acceptable' level of noise in one's own lesson but it is quite another to feel that 'talk' is passing straight through the paper-thin walls and invading the French lesson which is taking place next door. Noise and the ignoring of the elements of tradition are even more open to criticism if the school is 'formal' in structure. One has to co-exist with one's colleagues, and a public disagreement over conflicting basic philosophies is hardly conducive to harmony in the staffroom. A fellow teacher when asked what methods he used to encourage constructive talk in the classroom replied: 'I don't allow them to talk. My problem is making sure they don't talk.' His answer was intended to be humorous, but it contained an element of truth.

The pupils, too, have doubts about what is expected of them when they are confronted with a new situation. A plea for a discussion having been for so long one of the traditional ways of avoiding 'work' tends to relegate the discussion lesson, in the mind of the pupils, to a soft option, something not to be taken seriously, of little intrinsic value, perhaps a means of the teacher filling up thirty-five minutes without the chore of marking to follow.

In spite of all I have said so far, however, I suspect that most teachers of English see some place for oral work in the syllabus, and are fully cognizant of the social importance of talk and even recognize that discussion can crystallize the thought processes preparatory to the undertaking of some specified written assignment. Yet, even now, I suspect that most discussions in the classroom are teacher-led and teacher-dominated.

As the Bullock Report observes, whole-class teacher-led discussions tend to limit the available amount of discussion time for individual children.* This can have an inhibiting effect on some pupils, either because they do not have the opportunity to make a contribution to the lesson, or because they feel that the situation is a 'threatening' one, and they do not wish to seem foolish in what, for many of them, is a competitive situation.

Few adults would deny that talking in public is an ordeal even for those who are quite used to it, and for a shy or retiring child must be quite terrifying. As evidence of this, one has only to observe, at a public meeting, the reluctance that is often found to pose the first question to the speaker, or to recall the embarrassed, tongue-tied silence of a well-known footballer on being expected to 'say a few words' when receiving an award, even though he was quite used to performing on the field in front of thousands of critical spectators.

Reasons children talk in class
While project members shared the uncertainties expressed by their colleague quoted above, in the process of discussing and comparing their own experiences they became convinced that talk could and indeed did play an important part in their lessons. They were aware that children talk for a variety of reasons. Some of these are clearly inimical to the good conduct of a lesson, while others can be seen to help children to work.

On one occasion the project director sat and observed how children talked in an English lesson in one of the schools. He noted that the children had the task of filling in the blank map of an imaginary island with names of places and topographical details in preparation for writing a story about the island. They were a second-year, lower-band group of boys and girls. They were not talking all of the time; far from it: some were reading, some were writing, some were listening. But, when the need arose, they talked and the teacher allowed them to talk or, in some cases, stopped them according to his judgement as he monitored the children's progress.

The observer endeavoured to discover why the children and the teacher talked in that lesson. The reasons are illustrated in Figure 1. The teacher controlled the class by talking; children also controlled one another, some by listening, others by telling each other to be quiet and let them get on with their work. The teacher discussed one child's work, while other children discussed their own work in groups. One boy was reading his description of a desert island to another; a girl asked for a dictionary to

* *A Language for Life* (Report of Committee of Inquiry appointed by Secretary of State for Education and Science under chairmanship of Sir Alan Bullock), (HMSO, 1975).

look up a word; one boy, having learnt a new word, was saying it out loud to himself to celebrate the discovery; a girl was talking to herself while writing. In a corner, a girl called out because someone had taken her rubber; a boy near the window shouted because he needed attention.

Fig. 1 Some reasons why pupils and teachers talk in the classroom

The teacher of this class was not so complacent as to consider that he had created ideal conditions in his classroom, but the project director's observations helped him to realize that talk already had a valuable place in his classroom and that he need not worry about the compulsion felt by many teachers to stop children talking at all costs.

Project consultants
On the basis of similar early experiences, project members became aware of the need to translate their enthusiasm into a body of practical knowledge based on their individual work in each of their schools. Initially the group sought the assistance of Harold Rosen as consultant. Later they had the help of Douglas Barnes and Frankie Todd, whose research work done at the University of Leeds provided valuable back-up material, and whose personal assistance clarified project members' perceptions.

Relevance to the Bullock Report
At the same time as the project was starting, the Bullock Report was published, and this offered confirmation that the group was embarking on an investigation which had some value. The following topics, said the

report, needed to receive attention:

i   the effects of school and classroom organization on the pupils' language behaviour;

ii   the formulation into a coherent body of advice of the intuitions of teachers who are skilful at conducting discussions;

iii   the comparative achievements of small groups of pupils talking together (a) to a brief given by the teacher (b) without guidance; the most productive relationship between small-group and large-group work;

iv   the relationship of children's oral language ability to their reading and writing;

v   the effect of work in small groups of mixed ability on the language development of the less able (pp. 155–6).

In order to avoid quoting the Bullock Report at too great length here, its summary of conclusions and recommendations on talking and listening are set out in Appendix B.

Study of tape-recordings
With the five points from the Bullock Report in mind the group developed the following strategy. For the first year, project members decided to acquire as much experience as possible of the use of talk with their classes in the course of their normal teaching programmes. It was found to be valuable to make tape-recordings of children talking and to examine and discuss these recordings as a group. How these recordings were made, what methods of examination were used and suggestions which might help other teachers in the same process are contained in Appendix A. It was hoped that members of the project would be able to embark on specific studies relating to the use of talk during the second year based upon the bank of shared knowledge and experience built up during the first year.

Teachers as researchers
The raw material of the book consists mainly of tape-extracts made by teachers during the two-year life of the project. The special feature of these tape-recordings is that they were made by teachers who were part of the history and life of the schools in which they taught. Thus lessons were not specially set up for research purposes, but were part of the normal day-to-day experiences of the teachers and their classes. This, perhaps, could be seen as the main strength of the project: all contributing members were full-time teachers in comprehensive schools able to relate their observa-

tions and conclusions to their intimate knowledge of their pupils. Thus the situation was avoided in which researchers had to visit schools as 'strangers' to collect the data for their research.

The project team decided that they would attempt to build talk into their existing classroom practice, making modifications to teaching methods where these were felt to be needed. Once investigations were centred on existing rather than specially arranged lessons the team began to discover that children appear to have a latent ability to learn through talking and that this can be called upon in a multiplicity of ways as and when the need arises.

Project members' observations confirmed by project meetings
The project's own group interaction while talking about tapes made in lessons taught them much about group interaction in the classroom. Project members made the discovery that, after spending some time groping for a meaning, they would come to a moment of group consensus as if the dynamics of the group had created a meaning which individuals on their own might not have reached. It was possible to find the same sort of thing happening in children's talk. Another, minor but none the less important, discovery was that the group needed the occasional release from serious discussion, which a series of joking remarks provided, and that such joking often created the opening for a necessary change of direction in the discussion. Thus in the consideration of pupil talk they became more tolerant of what might appear to be irrelevant and light-hearted contributions.

Generalizations about talk from project data
From their work, project members gained a great deal of personal insight into the use of talk in their lessons. The aim of this book is to pass on some of these insights to interested teachers who wish to extend and develop the use of talk in their classrooms. It is not intended that the material in the book should present a series of firm conclusions and recommendations which can immediately be put into practice in any classroom to ensure the successful use of talk, but that it should encourage and help teachers to undertake their own investigations within the context of their own classes' interests and experiences. To this end the members of the project offer the following general observations based upon their common experiences:

1 To enable talk to take place effectively in the classroom the teacher has first to set up a relationship with the class in which he shows he

respects their judgement, is capable of uncertainty himself and is prepared to admit to being wrong. He needs to show them that he is prepared to allow them to work on their own, and is ready to accept that they can work well without his constant surveillance.

2 The teacher must accept the need to assert frequently that talk *is* of value or to imply by his method of talking to the children that this is so.

3 The teacher must not feel the need to indulge immediately in activities involving talk just because others do so, but should feel his way into using talk more effectively by means of a series of limited exercises: some examples of such exercises are given in Chapter V.

4 Activities involving talk should be introduced boldly and positively, never in a half-hearted way, since the latter is bound to generate a sense of insecurity in the children.

5 It must always be recognized that talk is only one of the ways in which learning can be helped to take place. Reading, writing and listening have their own necessary part to play in the process: talk can help as part of the whole learning process, complementing and adding new dimensions, but never detracting from the good of the whole.

These five observations lead on to a sixth which is in the form of an assertion showing that the intuitions with which the project members began their work were strengthened into a realization through practical experience and discussion. It complements similar assertions made by Douglas Barnes and Frankie Todd (made to us in conference and repeated in various forms in their publications) that using speech in the shaping of meaning is an important and valuable part of the learning process in schools. It is an assertion which cannot simply be taken out of context, however, and must be seen as being limited by points **1–5** above:

6 The project team considers that talk has a vitally important part to play in the secondary-school classroom, because the team's researches have clearly indicated that using speech in the shaping of meaning is a valuable element in the learning process.

Outline of the report
Chapter I, 'Starting-points: the first year of the project', illustrates the early work of the project and attempts to identify the body of knowledge and information which was built up as the result of project members sharing and discussing their work in the classroom. This chapter was written by Jon Pratt, and contains material from several schools.

Chapter II, 'Literature, the adolescent and small-group talk', concerns work done on teaching literature to fourth-year pupils in one of the project schools. That work was done by Tony Barry and Jon Pratt, and the chapter was written by them.

Chapter III, 'Talking and writing', arose out of the project work involving talk, done by third-year pupils in another of the project schools. It was written by Ian Graves who was responsible for the work.

Chapter IV, 'Differences between small-group talk and large-group talk', concentrates on the differences between pupils talking in groups of different size, as observed in a third school. The chapter was contributed by Nicholas Parsons.

Chapter V, 'Talk as part of the activity of learning', contains an anthology of material gathered from all the seven schools which were actually involved in the project. The chapter is intended to provide a series of ideas and suggestions illustrating some areas of the curriculum in which talk may be found to be a valuable teaching method. This chapter was compiled by the project director, Geoffrey Eggins.

Appendix A, 'Tape-recording, transcription and analysis: practical suggestions', gives guidance on methods of making tape-recordings, transcribing and analysing them, and is based on the experience of project members. Other appendices include the conclusions and recommendations on talking and listening from the Bullock Report and some useful references and classroom resources.

Conclusion

Taken as a whole, the book attempts to illustrate the experiences and work of a local curriculum development project, and the 'path of discovery' it followed. It is hoped that any discoveries revealed here will help and encourage other teachers to undertake the same journey themselves, and to make new discoveries as a result.

I. Starting-points: the first year of the project

As has been indicated in the Introduction, the first year of the project was spent gaining as much experience as possible in the use of pupil talk in the classroom. The material which resulted from this process formed a large number of tape-recordings and transcripts, together with the observation of the teachers concerned. By means of the close analysis and discussion of this material, the project built up a bank of shared knowledge and developed a certain expertise in the use of talk in the classroom and in the monitoring and assessment of children's performances. This in turn led to the position in which the project members could form a number of preliminary conclusions based on the evidence which had accumulated during the year. These conclusions were considered to be the basis for further, more specific programmes of work. This chapter attempts to illustrate the course of this process and to identify the conclusions which were the result.

It became clear to us at the outset that we could not hope to consider all the variables which might affect the use and effectiveness of pupils' talk. Our schools, for example, did not include an inner-city school nor a school with a significant immigrant population. We decided, therefore, to work with self-selected friendship groups of pupils rather than attempt to group pupils according to ability, sex or other categories. In short, we chose to set up those working situations which seemed most natural and practical in the classrooms of our schools and to concentrate our attention on what happened when children used talk in what was for them a secure and familiar framework. We leave it for other teachers to establish for themselves what combination of groupings would secure this framework in their own schools. Indeed, we would stress that our conclusions and recommendations relate to our own working set-ups and we have not attempted to establish a 'research situation' in which all possible variables have been considered. The analysis and commentary on our work is the subjective view of the group as a whole.

Our working brief as project members was to produce as much evidence as possible of pupil talk which arose naturally out of the normal course of our classroom work. After close analysis and study of the material a number of questions emerged. These questions related firstly to our role as teachers and secondly to what actually took place from the pupils' point of view during group talk:

1 *The teacher's role*

   a How important is the teacher's role in setting up and instigating talk activities?

   b What methods and techniques are available to the teacher to monitor, control and assess children's performance in group talk?

2 *The pupils' experiences*

   a What features of pupils' talk are unique in comparison with other learning/working activities?

   b What aspects of group talk can be identified as useful and valuable learning processes?

It soon became obvious, of course, that our observations relating to the work we had done covered a far wider area than our original questions had possibly allowed for. But in order to build up a body of practical knowledge it was felt they were a realistic basis upon which to establish our first conclusions. During the first year of the project, therefore, we used a large number of talk activities in our individual schools, tape-recorded groups at work and then studied as a group the transcriptions that were produced. The techniques of tape-recording, transcription and analysis are complex in themselves and are considered at some length in Appendix A. At this stage the type of material used and the tasks given were the choice of the individual teacher although there was extensive and valuable co-operation between individual project members.

As we used talk in our lessons, so we ourselves extended our own knowledge and expertise and by coming together as a group we attempted to share our individual experiences and to build up a bank of common knowledge and observations which arose from our combined practical work. It is this work which is the basis for the conclusions which we offer at the end of this chapter and for the work which is described in some detail in Chapters II, III and IV. It is obviously impossible to give details of all the material that was studied during this stage of our work. What follows are four representative examples of the material we studied with a summary of our analysis and findings. It is hoped that it can be seen how these findings led to our conclusions at the end of the chapter.

Examples of material used to stimulate discussion

a POP RECORDS

A group of third-year girls of slightly below average ability was played a selection of old pop records as a stimulus to group discussion. The records were: 'Tell Laura I Love Her', 'Moody River', 'Ebony Eyes', 'Endless Sleep', 'Green Green Grass of Home'.

The class was asked to divide into friendship groups and to talk about the records they had heard, saying whether or not they liked them and trying to identify a factor which they all had in common (in fact death features in all of them – a young boy killed in a stock car race, the suicide of a lovelorn girl, the death in a plane crash of a bride-to-be, another suicide, and, finally, the yearning to be home of a young man in the condemned cell). One group of four girls was sent into an adjoining classroom with a tape-recorder and the rest of the class adjourned to the corners of the English room.

The teacher hoped for:

a some sort of critical appraisal of the records;
b an idea of *why* young and old people like sad or sentimental songs;
c some discussion about the morality of suicide, and what motivates suicide attempts;
d a statement of attitudes towards capital punishment.

The tape-recording made of the girls' discussion in the adjoining room was disappointing to begin with, as the following extract shows.*

AMANDA Yeah/'Moody River' was a good record.
JOSEPHINE Oh yeah/but it was stupid of her hanging herself.
JILL Yeah/just 'cos film stars kill themselves/'cos it's too much hard work and that/don't they?
SARA Yeah/a lot of people do that.
JOSEPHINE Yeah/but it's a bit hard drowning yourself.
SARA I like the last/well not the last one.
ALL 'Ebony Eyes'.
AMANDA About getting married/but it was sad though/wasn't it?
JOSEPHINE A plane crash/you know/didn't expect it to happen.

* In all tape-extracts, fictitious names have been given to pupils.

This section is representative of much of the group's discussion. Opinions were given with little attempt to substantiate them with any sort of evidence and other members of the group appeared to be unwilling to question or challenge the views of others. In fact it would appear that the aim of the group was to work towards an easy consensus often based upon a number of received opinions. This consensus was frequently signified by the words 'It's stupid!' which occurred regularly in the girls' discussion. The girls seemed to perceive their task as being required to reproduce ideas and opinions which would be acceptable to their teacher rather than use talk as the opportunity to explore and express their own ideas and experiences. In the context of his original aims, the teacher naturally felt some degree of disappointment with what had actually resulted.

At this stage he felt that the failure of the group was probably the result of the way in which the activity had been set up and structured. Although the class showed enthusiasm for the material, the task given them for their talk lacked the structure of a number of specific questions or topics which would help to give their discussion direction and the security of a number of specified objectives. There is the danger, of course, in giving groups such a tightly structured task that there is no freedom for the exploration of their own ideas and they perform little more than an oral comprehension exercise. However, children of limited ability or who are inexperienced in the use of talk frequently need the security of a structured task which gives them clear objectives. With experience, groups then find it easier to go beyond the limitations posed by the task they have been given.

The teacher also felt that the stimulus material was too far removed from the girls' own direct experience and therefore they found it difficult to relate their own ideas to those received from the records. Without the foundation of ideas which connect with their own lives, children will very naturally fall back on the received opinions of others.

It can be seen, therefore, that the role of the teacher in setting up and instigating talk activity is a vital one and it would appear that, in this instance, it had a direct relationship with the success (or otherwise) of the group in the context of the teacher's original aims and intentions.

But there is great danger in looking at pupils' performance only in terms of the teacher's expectations. In group talk much that is valuable can occur irrespective of what the teacher intended or expected would happen. Project members soon learned not to judge children's performance in talk situations by the same criteria by which we judged other types of work – particularly writing. A later section of the transcript of the discussion showed this very clearly.

The girls have moved on to discuss, if only superficially, other forms of violence and violent death. Then, Jill introduced a personal anecdote into the discussion.

JILL I got followed by a man the other night when I was walking over to Youth Club.

(*Babble of general agreement/encouragement*)

AMANDA I don't like them/I'm scared.

JOSEPHINE Once I went/I was only about nine/with my brother/he was seven at the time/and I left my brother in Woolworth's/see/and this man/he was looking at the records/and this man comes up to him/and he says/are you alone/and my brother didn't know you see/and he goes yeah my sister's over there/you know/and this man/oh God/Steve walked out of the shop/and this man kept on following/you know/and said would you like to/like to/go into a shop and have a drink/and things like that/(*words inaudible*)/got out of/scared/as soon as I could/I was scared stiff.

SARA I was at the shops on the Bournville/and this man got out of his car/he goes do you want a sweet/and I goes no thank you/like that/and/er/he turned round/why not? and I said no I don't want to/and I started/I burst into tears and ran down into the . . .

AMANDA Oh/me and my sister were playing outside/and there was this man in a car/and he kept going past there/and he opened the window/and he said to me/do you want a sweet? and we says no thank you/and we go/no thank you/he says go on/and we goes we don't want one thank you/and he says go on/so we took a sweet and walked round the corner and threw it away.

JOSEPHINE Yeah.

AMANDA In case it was poisonous/you see.

JOSEPHINE Yeah.

In the form of a transcript, the significance of the above exchange can be easily overlooked. Teachers are accustomed to judging the written word by certain criteria such as range of vocabulary, sentence construction, sophistication of expression, etc. But in the assessment of group *talk* these criteria have little value. Josephine's anecdote was delivered with an immediate and vivid use of language which showed her awareness of an enthusiastic audience and the need to communicate clearly and dramatically to that audience. She built up a sense of suspense and tension within the group with considerable skill. Her breathless 'Oh God!' was used purely for dramatic effect. The success of her own anecdote encouraged Sara and Amanda to attempt their own.

It was the social interaction provided by the small group which provided the stimulus and motivation for Josephine's contribution. The presence of an immediate audience of her peers in the secure framework of a friendship group enabled Josephine to find and use the language and style necessary to recreate and communicate her original sense of fear and tension. Group talk here has the unique function of forcing children to test their statements against an immediate critical audience. Thus, if their statement is unclear, they will be challenged to rephrase it to make it clearer and if their anecdote is uninteresting or delivered in language which fails to bring it to life, they will lose the attention of their audience.

This example led us as a project group to realize that it is vitally important to look at the whole process taking place in a group discussion rather than to look merely at the outcomes or product in terms of the children's individual utterances. The value or interest of any one statement has to be related to the whole social interaction and learning process of the group. Douglas Barnes warned project members that it could be very misleading to judge the quality and analyse the nature of children's talk merely on the basis of a transcript, because in doing so one might be tempted to use linguistic criteria normally applied to written English, but inappropriate in the analysis of spoken English.

b PREPARING A TALK ABOUT UFOS
A third-year mixed-ability class in a different school had been told that they had to prepare a talk in groups to give to the rest of the class. The talk had to be on a topic of interest for which they had to collect their material beforehand. A group of four boys decided that their talk was going to be about UFOs. They thought the best way to go about it was to devise a questionnaire which they would put to people in the town, and were told by their teacher that they must be prepared to follow up differing responses to their questions. The group was observed by the project director, who did not take part in the discussion.

In the first of two half-hour lessons Paul, the most vociferous of the group, told the story of the time when *he* sighted a UFO.*

> 1 PAUL I was sitting on this haystack/I was sitting on the thing/and I looked over/I was just watching where the sun was setting/I could see the red rays just going out/and I was just looking/and then this/this/small light

---

* In tape-extracts throughout this book, utterances have been numbered only if reference is made to specific utterances in the commentary on an extract. Utterances are cited in the text by a number in square brackets. (When transcribing a complete tape-recording, utterances are normally numbered in sequence throughout the transcript – see Appendix A, p. 125.)

appeared/and then it got bigger and bigger/and bigger and bigger and bigger/seriously!

2 NEVILLE What colour was it?

3 PAUL Red.

4 NEVILLE Bright red?

5 PAUL Yeah/very bright red/much brighter than the red the rays were givin' off/I was looking at it and then it went that way/it went left and then it stopped and then it went right again.

6 NEVILLE Oh/Paul/you can't say left/it depends where you are/you've got to say north south east or west.

7 PAUL Well/it went north.

8 NEVILLE If it came over the sun it would have to be west.

9 PAUL I thought it was an aeroplane at first/but then I looked at it/and then it went up/and you know I thought/well/it could be that the aeroplane was a fast one/and then it went really fast/up and up/and then it stopped.

10 NEVILLE Did it go straight up?

11 PAUL Yes.

12 NEVILLE Aeroplanes can't go straight up.

13 PAUL Yes I know/that's what proves it wasn't an aeroplane.

14 NEVILLE It might have been a helicopter.

15 PAUL I doubt it.

16 NEVILLE Did it make any noise?

17 PAUL No/I couldn't hear it/it was about three million miles away.

18 NEVILLE Oh dear.

19 PAUL No/it was about ten miles away/I was going to get me camera but it went before I could get it.

It can be seen in this instance that the nature of the task given to the boys made it *essential* for them to talk, as the end-product of their work would represent them as a group and not individually. Therefore, they each had a commitment to share in and control the course of their progress. In many ways this is an ideal setting for effective small-group talk. The boys were also given quite clear objectives which in no way restricted the possible range and depth of their discussion but which did give them the security of a target to aim at.

In the example above, Paul offered a personal anecdote which related to the subject of their inquiry [1]. The presence of an immediate critical audience forced him first to develop and clarify what he said and then to defend his position against reasoned argument. Thus Neville [2] asked Paul for more information and having been given an answer which he felt was too vague [3] demanded that Paul be more specific [4]. Paul's answer was then far more detailed and included a useful distinction to help his audience visualize what he was attempting to describe. This process of assertion, challenge and restatement proceeded for the rest of the discussion. If the form of this process is somewhat aggressive in this example it is because it was natural for this group of boys – it was the social interaction they had created for themselves. (An extract from a later point in the discussion appears in Appendix A.)

Further unique features of group talk were identified from this example. It appeared that the framework of the group enabled and encouraged pupils to offer and set up hypotheses, ideas and experiences of their own for consideration and criticism by their peers. The valuable effect of this immediate audience was to make the boys extend, develop and articulate their ideas clearly. Thus, by finding the language to make their ideas clear to others, they were, at the same time, making their own learning more concrete for themselves. The finding of language to explain concepts and ideas is, in itself, a very valuable learning process and one which group talk would appear to encourage actively. In a written exercise or in the context of a class discussion it is doubtful whether many pupils would feel the need to extend, develop and define precisely their statements and ideas to this extent. The class discussion, to many children, is a barrier to confident expression and in a written exercise any critical presence, usually in the form of teacher comments, is too far removed to supply the type of pressure which a small group can place on its members.

Some children, it is true, are capable of the 'inner dialogue' which gives them the means constantly to question and reappraise their own ideas and statements. But this is a sophisticated skill requiring considerable intellectual motivation on the part of the child. The teacher can encourage this mental process in his pupils but usually only in the intimate and secure atmosphere of a 'one to one' relationship. The small group can, it would seem, help fulfil this function for the teacher, freeing him to play a more peripatetic role in the classroom. Thus the teacher must be prepared to delegate some of his authority, in the sense of the teacher as the arbiter of all learning activities and decisions in the classroom, to the small groups themselves. His task then is constantly to monitor and assess group progress, helping with whatever problems may arise.

c SONG LYRICS

Project members were interested to see if small-group talk would be an aid to children's learning not only in problem-solving and in the reception of new knowledge but in areas where a more aesthetic and interpretative response is required. This led to the use of small-group talk in the study of literature in an attempt to discover if talk would help children to appreciate and understand what they read and to relate the ideas and experiences received from literature to their own. This area is covered in considerably more detail in Chapter II.

In this example a group of third-year girls of high ability were given the lyrics of a Paul Simon song, 'The Sound of Silence'. After hearing the song they were asked to discuss together the following questions:

a   What is the writer's vision or dream? What do you think it means?
b   What is the 'neon light' and why do you think it became 'a god'?
c   Explain the paradox in the title of the song. What other paradoxes are there in the song and what is their purpose?
d   What do you think is the 'message' in the song? Is it one that you agree with?

It can be seen that the task was quite highly structured. This was because the group were relatively inexperienced both in group talk and in the close analysis of literature. The task was designed to give the girls security in that they had specific questions which gave them an approach to the song but it was also hoped that they would have sufficient freedom to explore their own ideas. The teacher was not particularly concerned about the children getting the questions 'right' or 'wrong' but more concerned that they would find ways of approaching and dealing with quite difficult tasks.

In the extract below, Janet read out question b and then quoted from the song:

1   JANET 'What is the neon light and why do you think it became a god?'
    'In restless dreams I walked alone
    Narrow streets of cobbled stone.
    Beneath the halo of a street lamp
    I turned my collar to the cold and damp
    When my eyes were stabbed by the flash of a neon light . . .'
2   KAY That's good/'and my eyes were stabbed'.
3   ALL Yeah.
4   JANET Oh yes/'split the night'/'the sound of silence'.
5   KAY This is all poetry/really.
6   JOY In a daze/really/instead of flashing lights/sorry.
7   KAY Well/this is all just a poem put to music/isn't it?
8   JANET Yeah.
9   JOY I know how it feels to feel a stab of light/though/because sometimes I go into the bathroom when I get out of bed/and it really hurts my eyes.
10 JANET Yeah/well/I said this morning when I came out of biology/I said/ Oh/isn't the sun strong?

11 JOY It's even brighter in the night/in the dark/when you get the light/and it does startle you.

12 JANET Yeah/I've noticed that.

13 JOY 'That split the night'.

14 KAY What is the neon light?

15 JOY 'That split the night'/isn't that good?

16 KAY Mmm/what is the neon light?

17 JOY Split the darkness.

18 JENNY Isn't that a sort of reddy light?

19 KAY Yeah/it's one of those great big bright lights.

20 JANET Yes I know.

21 JENNY But it means/it/sort of dizzy/it/sort of dizzy/and he's remembered back.

22 JOY No/I think it is really.

23 JANET Neon light/I think it became a god because it was light into his world of darkness/and he worshipped it perhaps/he worshipped the light.

24 KAY Oh yeah/yeah.

The girls' first reaction was one of simple aesthetic appreciation and enjoyment of the song; they shared together particular lines which had appealed to them. The act of speaking the lines out loud to a sympathetic audience as Kay did in [2] and Janet did in [4] is a form of celebration serving the purpose of deepening and cementing the speaker's own enjoyment while at the same time communicating it to others.

The next stage involved the relating of the images in the song to their own experience. Joy [9] said, 'I know how it feels to feel a stab of light,' and in those words initiated a vital part of the aesthetic and interpretative process – the vicarious identification with the ideas and experiences expressed in what she had read. Janet [10] participated in this process. At this point they were concerned with the physical experience of a bright light but the process of linking it with their own simple but striking experiences gave them a basis of understanding upon which Joy [13, 15 and 17] explored aloud the significance and striking qualities of the image 'split the night' and upon which Janet based her final interpretation of the poem [23].

In this one extract, therefore, a number of significant processes were taking place. The girls were articulating their aesthetic response to the song. They were relating their own experiences to those in the lyrics and they were using the evidence presented by the text *and* their own ideas and experiences to form hypotheses about the possible meaning and significance of the song.

Of course, we would hope or expect these processes to take place when we study any literature with older pupils, but are they always promoted by the teaching methods we use? In this example the children *constructed* ideas and knowledge by sharing their perceptions and experiences and as a group they acquired a collective responsibility for their own learning. Again the authority for making basic decisions in relation to their learning was removed, to a certain extent, from the teacher and invested in the group itself. If they failed to arrive at what the teacher may have conceived as the 'correct answer' they may well have succeeded in the far more important task of learning how to explore and come to terms with complex material and tasks.

It is noticeable that the social context of the group allows individuals to think aloud with confidence. Thus many of the statements in the above example serve the dual purpose of first clarifying the idea in the mind of the speaker and secondly of communicating that idea to others for their consideration and appraisal. Thus language serves the learning process on a number of different functional levels: it can be used to celebrate the enjoyment and aesthetic appreciation of literature; it can be a means of thinking aloud to clarify an individual's perceptions and ideas; and it can be used to communicate an idea to others.

d PICTURES OF AN EGYPTIAN TOMB

In the discussion of previous examples mention has been made of the role of the teacher in small-group talk. In the use of talk it is probable that the traditional role of the teacher in the classroom must change. In particular, the function of the teacher as the only or chief decision-maker in relation to the children's learning tasks and progress is removed. The teacher must delegate all or part of this authority and responsibility to the groups themselves.

But this does not mean that the teacher does not have a vital role to play. First, he must continually monitor and assess his pupils' progress and, secondly, he must offer a consultancy and advice service for those groups which have difficulties in carrying out their tasks or which require specific information. Both these tasks are probably best performed by direct teacher intervention in group talk.

The techniques employed by a teacher when joining a small group will obviously differ according to the personality of the teacher and his relationship with the children in his care. But it is vitally important that by his intervention the teacher does not give the group an easy shortcut to complete its task but gives the group the encouragement and confidence and guidance to complete the task by itself.

In the following example a first-year mixed-ability class in a humanities lesson had been given some pictures of an Egyptian tomb showing the mummy and various objects. The children were asked to decide why the objects, and especially the models and paintings, were in the tomb. The teacher noted that the use of small-group talk allowed the less able members of the class to work at their own pace and towards the end of the lesson he joined a group of less able girls to monitor and assess their progress.

1 TEACHER They believed that a person would need his body after he was dead, because he went on living.

2 SUSAN But what if the oil wore off?

3 TEACHER Well it did/yes mummies that are found today are all/a bit dried up.

4 JULIE Yeah/and parched.

5 TEACHER They're not perfectly preserved/they've still got skin on/but not perfectly preserved.

6 SUSAN Yeah/I know/but if they did survive how would they get out again?

7 TEACHER If they did . . .?

8 SUSAN If they did survive/if people did preserve them/how would they get into the . . .?

9 JULIE AND NATALIE (*Laughing*) Yeah!

10 JULIE Ah!

11 NATALIE Oh yeah! (*delighted*)

12 TEACHER That's a very good question.

This idea of the heavily bandaged mummy struggling to get out of its mummy-case revealed that these children had not fully grasped the nature of the concept 'afterlife'. The teacher continued as follows until light dawned.

13 TEACHER I think you can answer that by/if you look at the pictures on the wall.

14 NATALIE All people in his afterlife. (*laughter*)

15 TEACHER Now they would not be much good to him if they were pictures would they?/they would not be much good because . . .

16 SUSAN Reminding . . .

17 TEACHER A model of a boat would not be much good if it was a model/ this servant's wooden/he would not be much good/and you say he/the mummy/couldn't get up and walk around/well they didn't believe that the person would actually use the things there.

18 JULIE No/they believed that spirits did/didn't they!

19 TEACHER I think that's right.

The skill employed by the teacher here is obvious. The combination of explanation, questioning and praise guided the girls towards a fuller understanding of the subject. These, of course, are techniques employed by all teachers, but in the use of small-group talk they are particularly important. Here the teacher became in a sense a sympathetic member of the group helping the others to explore the problem rather than merely answering it for them. Thus he allowed Susan to put forward the all-important question [6 and 8] and gave her credit for it [12]. Then he resisted the temptation to answer the question for the children but guided them to a position from which Julie could triumphantly supply the correct answer. The teacher's carefully phrased approval 'I think that's right' [19] indicated his agreement not merely as 'the authority' but as a member of the group.

Within the security offered by a friendship group and under the cover provided by the 'noise blanket' from other groups, children are often far more prepared to admit their own misunderstandings and uncertainties and to ask questions to help solve their problems. Thus the teacher's task as guide and instructor of knowledge is made much easier. But he must be prepared to adapt and change his more traditional role in the classroom if this is to take place most profitably. Further examples of teacher intervention are given in Chapter IV.

CONCLUSIONS

The four examples given above are representative of the material members of the project were studying during the first year. We would not pretend that all the examples of pupil talk we collected offered such positive results. Many examples were disappointing for a number of different reasons. Often children seemed uncomfortable with the activity, self-conscious when faced by the tape-recorder and reluctant to commit themselves to any statement at all. Sometimes the social interaction created by a group was an over-aggressive and hostile one which precluded the free exchange of ideas.

But there are few teaching methods which do not have their crop of failures. The success of pupil talk is heavily dependent upon the motivation of pupils towards an activity which may be largely unfamiliar to them and which they may not recognize as 'work' in the traditional sense. The nature and stability of the relationship existing between teacher and class is also of vital importance. The teacher can only surrender authority and decision-making to his pupils on the basis of the security offered to both parties by an accepted working relationship. There are many other variables that may affect the success of small-group talk or, indeed, any other teaching method. Failures cannot be legislated against: practical experience is the major means of discovering how to avoid them.

We have felt the need to structure the use of small-group talk in teaching. Many may see this as rather artificial and would argue that talk should be allowed to arise naturally from whatever activity the children are engaged in and that any attempt to structure tasks or activities specifically for talk is to deny the natural benefits.

However, our aim has been to bring together a body of information which will be of value to teachers who wish to introduce some or more talk into their classrooms. Our experience has been that both teachers and pupils have needed the security and ordered approach offered by relatively structured activities and tasks. We consider that talk activities should be directly related to other activities in the classroom and that the idea of the 'oral lesson' is totally artificial, but they must also be identifiable and definable so as to afford the teacher every opportunity to monitor and assess his pupils' performance and progress. We believe that, in a sense, pupils have to be taught the value and techniques of talk as an activity in the classroom and we have found that a more informal, less structured use of talk is the result of continued practice and experience. Talk is both a teaching technique and a learning process which is at the disposal of all teachers, but like all teaching methods it can suffer from both overuse and misuse.

Conclusions from preliminary work

We offer the following conclusions from our preliminary work; it was from these conclusions that we proceeded with further work in our individual schools.

1 THE TEACHER'S ROLE

a The way the teacher structures and sets up the task or activity for talk has a direct relationship with the success or failure of the pupils, particularly when the pupils are inexperienced in the use of talk. The structure for the activity in the form of instructions or questions should offer the children a secure framework but should not be so restrictive that any form of exploratory thinking is curtailed.

b The recording of pupil talk and the study of subsequent transcriptions is the most effective method of monitoring and assessing performance. However, as the above method is very time-consuming, the teacher will more often rely on his intuitive assessments formed by intervening in group talk. This intervention can serve the dual purpose of supplying the teacher with information about the groups' progress and also of helping and guiding groups with problems. Effective teacher intervention demands that the teacher abdicates what may be his normal classroom role as chief authority and decision-maker and takes over what may be described as a consultancy role.

2   THE PUPILS' EXPERIENCES

a   *Unique features of group talk*
In our view group talk is a unique learning activity for the following reasons:

i   It provides a secure social framework within which even reluctant children are likely to feel able to make a contribution.

ii   It provides an immediate critical but acceptable audience which encourages children to:
   (*a*) offer their ideas, opinions and anecdotes for appraisal and acceptance;
   (*b*) clarify, extend and develop their statements to meet and satisfy the criticism and questioning of their peers;
   (*c*) develop their language skills to ensure effective communication of their ideas;
   (*d*) be willing to offer challenge to the views of others and to accept challenge to their own views;
   (*e*) develop the ability to compromise and to form a consensus of views.

iii   It encourages children to take responsibility for their own learning and to take decisions regarding their own progress and methodology.

b   *Learning experiences*

i   The learning experience of children engaged in group talk is directly related to the social interaction of the group. Any judgements as to the value of the experience must be based not only on individual utterances by members of the group but also upon the knowledge or learning created by the group constructing knowledge together. Thus individual utterances are not end-products in their own right but components in the group's experience understanding.

ii   Judgements of performance in group talk must not be based upon the criteria used for assessing pupils' written work. Effective communication in relation to immediate audience is possibly the best criterion.

iii The following is a summary of the major learning experiences which can be offered to children engaged in group talk:

(*a*) the experience of exploratory thinking within a free and flexible framework as opposed to the learning of received knowledge or information;

(*b*) the experience of constructing ideas and knowledge as a group activity in order to form an agreed consensus;

(*c*) the experience of being able to think aloud in order to clarify and develop ideas and hypotheses;

(*d*) the experience of being forced to find their own language to articulate their ideas and concepts as opposed to merely adopting the language of others;

(*e*) the experience of developing their own methodology to handle various tasks and problems.

iv The process of talking together in small groups is its own product. Thus, we should look not so much at what learning the group has acquired in terms of new information, but at what it has acquired in terms of learning skills in the process of learning through talking.

II. Literature, the adolescent and small-group talk

Literature brings the child into an encounter with language in its most complex and varied forms and is a valuable source of imaginative insight. It should be recognized as a powerful force in English teaching at all levels.

Exploratory talk by the pupils has an important function in the process of learning.

A Language for Life
(Bullock Report, HMSO, 1975)

This chapter sets out to describe how two members of the project team, colleagues in the English department in one of the schools in Woodspring, worked on a problem area in their own curriculum and teaching, using the resources of the project to help them analyse and evaluate their work.

Two basic problems were dealt with:

i pupils' transition from reading children's literature to studying adult literature;

ii how to teach literature to the adolescent.

The chapter demonstrates some of the solutions they found to the problems, which involved the use of talk in small groups as the central element. The main aim of the work was to attempt to establish to what extent small-group talk is a valuable learning process.

The pupils concerned were in the fourth year of an 11–16 comprehensive school of approximately 1250 children. Two groups were used: one a high-ability, potential GCE O-level group, the other group containing the full CSE range. Both groups comprised twenty-seven pupils.

The groups were asked to tackle material which placed a greater demand on their language skills, understanding and maturity than anything they had studied previously. They were asked to explore fully the themes and ideas expressed in what they read, and to compare the understanding of the material with their own and their contemporaries' ideas and experiences. In a sense this was an introduction to adult literature, and the examples of work that follow show children's early attempts at using talk in this new area for them. It was hoped that these first experiences would help them to develop their skills and abilities in the future.

It has been shown that children go through stages of development in the use of talk before reaching the age of adolescence when, in Jean Piaget's words, they begin to show 'the capacity to reason in terms of verbally stated hypotheses and no longer merely in terms of concrete objects and their manipulation . . .' Piaget goes on to say:*

> . . . this is a decisive turning-point because to reason hypothetically and to deduce the consequences that the hypotheses necessarily imply (independent of the intrinsic truth or falsehood of the premises) is a formal reasoning process. From the social point of view there is also an important conquest. Firstly, hypothetical reasoning changes the nature of discussions; a fruitful and constructive discussion means that by using hypotheses we can adopt the point of view of the adversary (although not necessarily believing it) and draw the logical consequences it implies. Secondly, the individual who becomes capable of hypothetical reasoning, by this very fact will interest himself in problems that go beyond his immediate field of experience.

It is because children are capable of expanding and developing their intellectual abilities in this way that we concentrated on the fourth year of the secondary school. Perhaps one of the main reasons for studying literature at this age is to help children to move just beyond their own experience and into the beginnings of an adult world in which they show curiosity. Literature offers children a representation of experience which can then be compared with their own. If this is to have any benefit the children must be given every opportunity to extend and develop their own thinking abilities.

The importance of literature in the teaching of senior pupils can be summarized as follows:

i   it offers a means of conveying experiences which overlap with those of the pupil;

ii it helps to project children into areas just beyond their own experience;

* See J. Piaget, 'Intellectual evolution from adolescence to adulthood' (translated by J. Bliss and H. Furth), *Human Development*, vol. 15 (1972), pp. 1–12.

iii it provides an environment in which individuals can test their own
ideas against those of others;

iv it acts as a stimulus to their ability and desire to theorize and hypo-
thesize.

However, the concern of education in the upper end of the secondary
school is often that children should learn, in the sense of the memorizing,
recall and presentation of information. This is not helped by the pressures
of external examinations. It means that when children are at the stage of
developing the capacity for thinking theoretically, we may give them less
and less opportunity to do so. There can be an exaggerated reliance on
children's writing to assess their ability, and a dependence on instruction
and learning by rote to improve their performances. Thus, often the concern seems to be with the product rather than the process of learning –
developing children's ability to reproduce accurately information which
has been acquired is given more emphasis than developing their ability to
think theoretically and form and test their own hypotheses.

This situation would seem to work against what teachers would regard
as the importance and value of the teaching of literature. It means that
literature is often used purely as illustrative material, which restricts rather
than expands the range and quality of the pupils' understanding. The
demands of external examinations can lead the teacher to use the methods
of direct instruction, with emphasis upon such things as character notes
and scene summaries which encourage children to reproduce received
opinion, and not to develop their own. This may help the pupils to pass
examinations (and we would recognize the importance of that) but does
not lead pupils to a deeper and more satisfying understanding of their
reading. The assessment of children's understanding relies heavily upon
literal comprehension, and far too infrequently moves into the areas of
inferential and evaluative comprehension which encourage pupils' own
critical thinking.

Our belief is that children should be given the opportunity for their own
thinking. In the context of normal classroom procedures this is possibly
difficult to achieve. The presence of a teacher in itself will tend to inhibit
and constrain the freedom of children to explore fully their own ideas.
Douglas Barnes argues for pupil participation in the thinking process:*

Here lies the importance of pupil participation. It is when the pupil is required
to use language to grapple with new experience, or to order old experience in

* See Douglas Barnes *et al.*, *Language, the Learner and the School* (Penguin
Books, 1969, revised edition 1971), p. 61.

a new way that he is most likely to find it necessary to use language differently. And this will be very different from taking over someone else's language in external imitation of its forms: on the contrary, it is the first step towards new patterns of thinking and feeling, new ways of representing reality to himself.

Also, it is our belief that by talking in small groups children can achieve the level of participation and the freedom of thought that enables them to use language that leads them to understanding. By the use of talk in small groups it is possible that children, in Douglas Barnes' words, will '. . . develop their own learning strategies . . .', will be able to compare their own views with those of others, test their hypotheses and constructions against a variety of evidence and thus develop the ability to think. They will be forced to perform these operations not with the teacher as the central authority and supplier of 'correct answers', but on the basis of their own co-operation in the process of talk and discussion.

In the study of literature at this stage in the secondary school small-group talk would seem to provide a secure framework in which the pupil can:

i   articulate his own response to what he has read;

ii   relate that response to the response of others;

iii identify the relationship between literature and his own experience;

iv   extend his own experience by the full understanding of what he reads, and the understanding achieved by others;

v   develop his own skills of critical thinking;

vi   develop learning strategies within the group which enable him to handle difficult material.

What follows is only a small selection of work related to the use of small-group talk in the teaching of literature. We used self-selected friendship groups of four or five pupils, usually of the same sex. Perhaps we were fortunate in that we had at our disposal a number of suitable areas outside the classroom for group talk, enabling us, if required, to tape two or three groups each session, though children do not need to leave the room in order to take part in talk activities. In all cases the teacher was absent during group talk, but intervened occasionally to assist pupils in their task and to monitor their progress.

It was not our intention to set up a 'research situation' from which firm and demonstrable conclusions could be drawn; rather our intention was to describe our observations in the context of the normal work within the department. What we hope to show by looking closely at examples of pupils talking are the skills and strategies they can demonstrate when dealing with a variety of tasks. Our examples include talk related to song lyrics, plays and poems.

We do not pretend that the tape extracts reveal great levels of insight into the materials the children are studying, but we consider that they show that the children are mastering techniques which will enable them to develop their critical faculties further than would otherwise have been possible.

a Questions on song lyrics

Because children need to be encouraged to realize that talk is an important and necessary part of the learning process, and have to be brought gradually to the stage where they can develop hypothetical reasoning powers, inexperienced groups need the security of a structured framework in which to articulate their views; yet that framework must be one which makes demands on their ability to think and understand.

The structured framework in this case was provided by songs from the album *Bookends* recorded by Paul Simon and Art Garfunkel (CBS 63101). The song 'Save the Life of My Child' is about a boy who commits suicide by jumping from a building, and the reactions of the people watching the incident; 'America' tells of a young man who is 'lost' and sets off to find America and himself; 'Overs' deals with love which has gone wrong, but which still seems a habit hard to break; 'Old Friends' and the title song, 'Bookends', give visions of the desolation and loneliness of old age.

It was felt that the songs were difficult in that each one contained a theme which was not always stated explicitly and the songs were all linked thematically, although this link could only be identified by the understanding of the individual songs. At the same time, hearing the songs offered an immediacy of impact not offered by traditional poetry and provided a connection with the pupils' own culture and experience.

The questions were designed not as literal comprehension but as routes the children could take to investigate the meaning and theme of each song. It was hoped that the groups would show willingness to explore fully the implications of each question and that they would demonstrate skills of selection from their reading in order to articulate their conclusions precisely. The pupils were played a tape of the songs with a copy of the lyrics in front of them, and were given the questions without further explanation, except that it was made clear that the questions were not intended for written answers. Thus, the teacher's emphasis was placed upon talk as the 'work' for the lesson.

The following questions were given to the pupils:

1 'Save the Life of My Child'

   a What is the attitude of the various spectators towards the boy? Do you think they care about what happens to him?

   b Why do you think the words of the mother are repeated three times in the song? What does this show about the attitude of the crowd towards the incident?

   c What do you think the boy means when he says 'Oh, my Grace, I got no hiding place'? Suggest possible reasons for his suicide.

   d Do you think that this song has anything to say in general about the attitude of adults towards young people?

2 'America'

   a Make up characters for the two people in the song. Give their ages, family backgrounds, brief histories, etc.

   b Can you suggest what the boy might mean by 'I've come to look for America' other than just travelling around looking at the sights like a tourist?

   c In what sense do you think the boy is 'lost'?

3 'Overs'

   a How old do you think the people in this song are?

   b What is 'the game' and why is it 'over'?

   c Why don't the couple split up?

4 'Old Friends'

   a Why are the old people described as 'bookends'?

   b What impression of old age does the song give?

   c What is the 'same fear' in the last verse?

5 'Bookends'

   a What 'time' is the song talking about?

   b Why do you think the song is titled 'Bookends'?

6 General

These songs are all about different stages in our lives from youth to old age. Looking at the songs, what do you think the writer considers to be the differences and similarities between the different ages?

One group of four girls from the CSE class produced a very encouraging tape. It was noted how enthusiastically they approached the work, and they were offered frequent praise and encouragement. The following is an extract from their talk which concerns question 1c.*

1 MARIA The next one.	Chairman stating time to move from one completed task to the next.
2 ROSEMARY What do you think the boy means when he says 'Oh, my Grace, I got no hiding place'?	Adopts chairman's role and reads the question. The chairman's role is being shared.
3 JENNIFER He's got no home to go to?	Setting up hypothesis for consideration by the others. Uttered in the form of a question.
4 CHARLOTTE No. 5 MARIA No.	Initial rejection of hypothesis.
6 MARIA He's got a home/'cos he's got his mother.	Evidence from the song to support the rejection.
7 JENNIFER Yeah/well/they might be out on the streets/squatters ...	Hypothesis modified in the light of the objection.
8 CHARLOTTE They could/ooh! 9 JENNIFER Sorry!	Irrelevant interruption – tape-recorder knocked.
10 ALL (*Laughter*)	
11 MARIA I got no hiding place/that might mean ...?	Goes back to quotation, thinking aloud.
12 JENNIFER He wants a hiding place/ and he hasn't got one.	Jennifer takes up Maria's thinking.
13 CHARLOTTE (*Laughter*)	
14 MARIA He doesn't like people.	Maria extends the idea – still thinking aloud to herself.
15 ALL (*Laughter*)	
16 MARIA He doesn't like people really/you know he just doesn't like people.	Articulates it to the others as a solution.
17 CHARLOTTE He's got nowhere to go to/no one to run to.	Agrees with Maria's conclusion.
18 JENNIFER No.	

* The extract is given in the form of single parallel comment on individual utterances (see Appendix A).

19 MARIA He hasn't got any friends. ⎫
20 JENNIFER He wants to get away from it all. ⎪
21 MARIA You know he hasn't got any friends. ⎬ Supportive restatements of a mutually agreed conclusion.
22 JENNIFER He hasn't got a hiding place/so he can't get away from it all/like. ⎪
23 CHARLOTTE He hasn't got a place where he can get away from it all. ⎭

24 MARIA Great! ⎤ Very brief statement of success and satisfaction.

The following general points emerge:

i   The social interaction of the group allowed individual members to adopt the role of chairman and thus the group was not dominated by one personality.

ii Individuals were prepared to state their own ideas and hypotheses for the consideration and criticism of others – Jennifer [3].

iii The pressure of an immediate audience encouraged pupils to reconsider and amend their ideas – Jennifer [7].

iv Pupils were encouraged to think aloud – Maria [11] and [14]. This enabled others to assist them to develop and articulate their ideas – Maria [16].

v   When an agreed conclusion was found all members of the group showed their acceptance by supportive restatements (in utterances [20]–[23] it was noticed that there was an increase in the pace and clarity of expression).

At the end of their talk there is evidence that the group had been successful in relating their understanding of the individual songs to form a concluding generalization. This is shown in the following extract which is concerned with the final question.

MARIA 'These songs are all about different stages in our lives from youth to old age. Looking at the songs, what do you think the writer considers to be the differences and similarities between the different ages?'
CHARLOTTE The difference/he said differences first.
MARIA Well/the young people seem more adventurous/don't they?
JENNIFER Yeah/they want to do more/and the old people do nothing.
MARIA The old people they just sat there doing/thinking of what they were going to do/but they . . .

JENNIFER Yeah/and they were sort of sitting on a park bench all the time.
MARIA Bookends.
JENNIFER Thinking of their memories.
CHARLOTTE Yeah.
MARIA Thinking of the past/of what they should have done/they could have done.
JENNIFER Yeah/what they could have done/what they might have done.
MARIA What's the similarities then?
JENNIFER Loneliness.
MARIA Oh yes/'cos the first one . . .
ROSEMARY Yeah.
MARIA None of them seem very happy do they?
JENNIFER He committed suicide didn't he?
MARIA Yeah/in that one.
JENNIFER And then . . .
CHARLOTTE None of them seem very happy.
JENNIFER They/they would go off to America/to find America.
CHARLOTTE Yeah.
JENNIFER What about 'Overs'?
CHARLOTTE They're not very happy/are they?
JENNIFER And then 'Old Friends'/their loneliness and thinking and things.
MARIA Last one was the same.
CHARLOTTE Yeah.

Again it is noticeable that the pupils constructed ideas by a process of connecting individual contributions to form a group understanding.

Though the material was chosen deliberately as an introduction to this type of activity, it is obvious that any other songs of a similar type could be chosen. What is important is that the material should be both challenging and readily identifiable for the pupils, and that the tasks set should be structured enough to give security, and yet should enable the pupils to develop their own ideas. If the task is too vague the result will be repetition and weak generalization, but if it is too rigidly structured the pupils will merely perform an oral comprehension exercise, very rarely moving from the literal response. It is only with extensive experience that pupils are able to approach literature without guidance, and to form their own questions.

b Thematic work on adolescence and adult life: CSE literature

It was decided that the CSE group would follow a thematic approach to adolescence and adult life in the hope that this would give them an overall structure from which they would gain the experience and confidence to tackle tasks with less guidance from the teacher.

To achieve this end it was hoped that the themes chosen would be of immediate interest to them and that they would, as the Bullock Report says, offer 'valuable opportunities [to] extend and not restrict the range and quality of the pupils' experience of literature'. It was an approach new to the pupils and the teacher, and required the searching out and production of suitable material. The length of treatment of each theme was left flexible in order not to impose too strict a time limit on their talk, though in practice it was found that they would talk profitably for between half an hour and three-quarters of an hour. For some of the themes they needed to have two or three talk sessions. The themes covered included: The Problems of Adolescence, Violence, Sex, Marriage, The Family, Work, Old Age and Death. These are topics that occur very often in fourth-year work and in literature read by them in that year, and are subjects that pupils usually want to discuss, though the quality of discussion often varies a great deal, particularly if conducted in a large group. It is inevitable that at this age-level literature will contain contentious and controversial issues, but a secure relationship with the teacher and the freedom offered by small-group talk provides pupils with the opportunity to think seriously about them.

A variety of material was used when considering the theme of sex, including that in *The Urge to Mate* by T. H. Parker and F. J. Teskey, extracts from *A Kind of Loving* by Stan Barstow and a poem by Brian Patten called 'Party Piece'.* The extracts were chosen because of their different styles and content, and it was hoped that pupils would make sense of those differences.

The groups were asked to work out their own approach to the extracts – considering one at a time or all together. They were to have the following points in mind:

i   The attitude of the people involved.
ii   The way the experience is conveyed, i.e. the language of the extract.
iii What is being said about the value of the experience?
iv   Which comes closest to your idea of physical love, and why?
v   How do they compare with other ideas of love you have read or heard?
vi   Should you be reading them at all? Should extracts like these be an important part of any sex education programme?

* Publication details of the books and poems mentioned in the text are given in Appendix C.

Although by this time the class had tackled two or three themes by talking in small groups it was felt that they still needed a fairly structured task in order to give them the security in which to work effectively. The extracts provided a common ground outside themselves from which they could develop and articulate their personal views and experiences. However, it can be seen that the pupils were being given more flexibility and a looser structure than they had with the work on *Bookends,* and there was a progressive relaxing of the structure as they worked through the themes so that by the end they were attempting to devise and answer their own questions, and doing so quite competently.

Pupils were given a copy of the extracts and questions, and these were then read to them by the teacher. Two groups were to record their talk and were sent off to other areas; the rest remained in their groups in the classroom.

The two groups who recorded their talk produced very different tapes, but both are interesting for the response to the material and the way it was approached.

The four girls in the *Bookends* transcript have progressed well, and have developed the skill of reflexivity – 'the ability to monitor [one's] behaviour so as to adjust and modify [one's] strategies'.*

1 CHARLOTTE 'Work out your own group approach to these three extracts – either take one at a time . . .'/shall we do that?

2 ALL Yeah.

3 CHARLOTTE '. . . and examine it, or talk about it all at once. Discuss them with the following considerations in mind: one, the attitude of the people involved.'

4 JENNIFER What's the first one?

5 CHARLOTTE *A Kind of Loving* by Stan Barstow.

6 MARIA They both want it/don't they?

7 ALL (*Laughter*)

8 CHARLOTTE 'The attitude of the people involved'/well/they both want it.

9 MARIA They both love each other.

10 JENNIFER Yeah.

11 MARIA He loves her even more afterwards.

12 CHARLOTTE Yeah!/what's the next one?/'The way the experience is conveyed, i.e. the language of the extract'/what's that mean?

13 MARIA This one's more realistic/isn't it?

14 CHARLOTTE Yeah/easy to understand.

15 MARIA It's more modern/actually/isn't it?

* See D. Barnes and F. Todd, *Communication and Learning in Small Groups* (Routledge & Kegan Paul, 1977).

16 JENNIFER You can understand it more easily than that one.
17 CHARLOTTE Yeah/more realistic/yeah.
18 MARIA More modern isn't it?
19 JENNIFER More up-to-date/it's easier to understand/it's got words that we know/we understand.
20 MARIA Not like that one.
21 CHARLOTTE We're not on that one yet/all right/all right/we're not talking about that one yet/shut up/'What is being said about the value of the experience?'
22 MARIA Makes them love each other more/doesn't it?
23 CHARLOTTE Yeah.
24 MARIA Afterwards.
25 CHARLOTTE Anything else to say about that?/no?
26 JENNIFER Oh come on/we want to describe them in detail.
27 CHARLOTTE Come on then!
28 MARIA Can't we just talk about them all?
29 CHARLOTTE Just talk about it in general then/all right/talk about all of them.

The approach was decided at the beginning and immediately they set about the task. They were so intent on getting on with the work that they resisted the temptation of consequent irrelevance after distracting laughter at Maria's frank statement at [6] and she went on to develop her point at [9] and [11]. They made some important points about the language of the extract in the conversation that followed [13 to 20].

Charlotte realized that they had moved on to the next extract without finishing the first and demanded order for the next question [21]. Having answered the question she acted as chairman again and asked for any more contributions before they moved on to the next question.

At this point two important things occurred:

i   Jennifer [26] realized that she was dissatisfied with what had been done so far, in that she felt they had been performing an oral comprehension: stating the question, finding a simple answer and being satisfied with that. She wanted more 'detail': she wanted them to talk more and thus explore all the possibilities. It is exactly this approach and critical awareness of their own performance that one hoped would develop.

ii Maria [28] thought that the problem might be the way they had set about the task; they should have discussed them all together (in fact, it should be admitted that the questions were phrased deliberately so that they favoured the more general approach). The ease with which Charlotte accepted Maria's comment would suggest they had all felt this way, and it was encouraging that they were thinking about the strategies they were using in their work, and the appropriateness to the task in hand. From this point on the discussions improved considerably.

Towards the end of the tape they became involved in relating these extracts to their own and others' experiences, and showed perception and honesty in their comments, gaining confidence from each other.

1 JENNIFER 'Which comes closest to your own idea of physical love, and why?'
2 CHARLOTTE Oh!
3 MARIA The first one I think.
4 JENNIFER Yeah/the first one.
5 MARIA It's more realistic/the same as your age isn't it?
6 CHARLOTTE Yeah/I mean that one/I/that would be someone older I reckon. (*referring to another extract*)
7 MARIA Not older/but more sophisticated.
8 CHARLOTTE I reckon older.
9 MARIA The last one though/that would be for people who maybe married young.
10 CHARLOTTE Not necessarily.
11 JENNIFER Well why not/because people/somebody who is experienced/very well experienced/that is you know ...
12 MARIA Prostitute?
13 JENNIFER Yeah/I s'pose/who keeps having affairs/not necessarily prostitutes.
14 CHARLOTTE Yeah/just go/you go to a party and/go there just for one thing.
15 MARIA 'Cos if you were married you could do things like that/just a one day sort of thing.
16 CHARLOTTE Oh!!
17 JENNIFER Ugh!!
18 MARIA He could!/it's easy enough/what about the next one?
19 JENNIFER Have we answered that question?
20 ROSEMARY 'How do they compare with other ideas of love you have read or heard?'
21 MARIA Different/it's very different.
22 CHARLOTTE Different.
23 JENNIFER I mean when you hear about other kinds of love it's all sort of four letter words isn't it/and all sort of slang they say it in/and this book it was brought out nice you know.
24 CHARLOTTE Yes/how romantic can you be?
25 JENNIFER The man here remarks.
26 ROSEMARY Yeah/gentle.

27 MARIA It never works out the same though does it?/you read all these stories and then you . . .

28 CHARLOTTE Yeah/well. (*laughs*)

29 JENNIFER There are stories everywhere about people/sort of/ah/they um . . .

30 CHARLOTTE Come on/you've got to say it/because you can't put face expressions on the tape Jenny.

31 MARIA No/but when you do/say/it's not the same is it?

32 JENNIFER It's all sort of slangy.

33 CHARLOTTE When you do what?

34 JENNIFER That's sort of to say . . .

35 MARIA No/but you didn't/you expect more/I did/but I . . .

36 JENNIFER Pardon?

37 MARIA I expected more.

38 CHARLOTTE What do you mean?/if you read or if you do it?

39 MARIA Look/if/when I read about it/right?

40 JENNIFER Mmmmm.

41 MARIA It seems more than it is.

42 CHARLOTTE Yeah/like they make it sound all perfect like.

43 MARIA Yeah/but it isn't.

44 CHARLOTTE No.

45 MARIA Is it?

46 CHARLOTTE Things can go wrong.

47 ALL (*Laughter*)

48 MARIA No/but it isn't/is it?

49 CHARLOTTE No.

50 MARIA I don't think it is/it's not as exciting.

51 CHARLOTTE They make it sound right/sort of perfect/perfect situations and . . .

52 MARIA Yes.

53 CHARLOTTE And lovely.

54 MARIA And nothing to do.

55 JENNIFER Nothing'll happen.

56 CHARLOTTE Yeah/she's got nothing else to do/except make love and have sex.

57 MARIA It doesn't work out that way does it?

Nearly all the groups felt the same as Maria [3] about which extract they could identify with most easily, and which was the most sophisticated and the most 'romantic'.

It was pleasing to see they felt the extracts were better than many of the things they had read – Jennifer [23]. Though with remarkable honesty, Maria, in the final section, said that literature she had read had little in common with her own experiences. She picked up Jennifer's thoughts [29] and had the confidence to go on and articulate them [35, 43, 48, 50, 57]. There was a short discussion later as to whether this section should be left on the tape, and they all thought it important and relevant enough to be left.

The discussion moved on to considerations of sex before marriage, the age of consent, contraception and rape. The important factor was that the focal point of the extracts and task had given them a common ground from which they could start to develop their own thoughts and to which they could return. Far too often pupils are given a topic to discuss, with nothing to provide the springboard for discussion, whereas here it grew naturally out of the work they were given to do. In fact the girls made the point themselves:

CHARLOTTE Why shouldn't you read those books?/you know it's not going to harm you/is it?/I mean.

MARIA You'd know more about life then/and more about what to expect.

JENNIFER Yeah/you've got to find out about things/and the best thing about reading is if you don't understand you can ask.

CHARLOTTE It can't harm you/I mean not reading it on your own/it'd be different if we saw films on it.

ROSEMARY Yeah.

CHARLOTTE But I can't see any harm in reading it.

MARIA I know/but what about at school?/do you think we should do some at school?

CHARLOTTE Well it's a bit embarrassing at times/for some people it is.

ROSEMARY I'd be embarrassed to go into a shop and buy a book like that.

MARIA Yeah/so would I.

CHARLOTTE Yeah/well like in social studies you've got to do about abortion and Mr Jones wanted to talk about it/but . . .

MARIA I know/it's a bit difficult to talk about it/isn't it?

CHARLOTTE Oh we haven't done that yet.

MARIA Embarrassed in trying to . . .

CHARLOTTE You sort of . . .

ROSEMARY And you know you can't really sit and talk about that.

There is no doubt that this group of girls became very competent in the use of talk, both in their method and content. Their efforts can be compared with those of a group of three boys who struggled with the tasks, and continued to perform oral comprehensions for the most part. Even so, there were glimpses of insight that they could have developed had they not been so eager to find an answer and move on. They had a lively discussion, but usually it remained at a literal and rather superficial level.

1 KEITH Shut up a minute/that bit is like a sort of climax of it.
2 SEAN Yeah/it is.
3 SIMON But it doesn't say anything about people/I reckon they should get to know real people/and what the people feel like/it doesn't say anything about the people.
4 KEITH Yeah/it's all sort of complicated words.
5 SEAN I suppose that the first one is the beginning/that's the middle and that's the end.
6 KEITH No/you idiot.
7 SIMON No!
8 KEITH 'The way the experience is conveyed, i.e. the language of the extract.'
9 SIMON Well/this one's stupid really/the language/there's nothing in it at all/really.
10 KEITH They wouldn't say that sort of thing to each other/would they?
11 SIMON I reckon that one's more to the point/more like it/so you understand it better.
12 KEITH Yeah/more basic.
13 SIMON I like the first one/that was brilliant that was/I enjoyed it.
14 KEITH 'What is being said about the value of the experience?'/I think there's a lot being said about the value of it/'cos it goes into every detail/ don't it?
15 SIMON Well . . .
16 KEITH Well/it doesn't actually go on about sex.
17 SEAN Well/well it does a bit.
18 SIMON But it could be something else if you really put your imagination to it/you could say it was anything/but the other one makes sure that they are people/like where it gets to that 'harnessing' and all that/that's pretty obvious what that is.

The following points emerge from the tape extract:

i   Like the girls, this group of boys chose to take one extract at a time, but, unlike the girls, did not realize the limitations of that approach and continued with it, though making comparisons between the extracts – Simon [11, 13 and 18].
ii   They did move towards a consideration of imagery, but it was quickly dismissed as unrealistic, and not what real people would say – Simon [9, 11 and 18].
iii They were quick to come to group conclusions, either in agreement Keith and Simon [9, 10, 11, 12] or disagreement – Keith and Simon [6 and 7]. But they never restated their consensus before moving to the

next question: the decision to move on seemed quite arbitrary – Keith [8 and 14].

iv The hypotheses put forward were not developed because they had neither the confidence nor competence to do so. Sean's idea [5] was easily and hastily crushed, and Keith was about to make a very serious point [14] but quickly dropped it when Simon [15] questioned it with 'Well . . .' In fact he almost contradicted himself [16] in order to be in agreement.

Even so, towards the end of their talk they were struggling towards a serious look at style, and there were signs of co-operative learning from the stating, developing and testing of hypotheses, though they rarely managed to take them far enough, or refer to their own experiences.

Generally, the treatment of this theme by all the groups was encouraging and suggested that the class as a whole was starting to assume the attitude that talk was an important part of their work. This was confirmed by the way they approached and handled later themes.

c Shakespeare and contemporary plays and poems: O-level literature

Less freedom in terms of material and methods was possible with the O-level group, and in the work they did there were quite specific intentions which related to the academic demands of the O-level English literature examination. It was hoped that the use of small-group talk would assist pupils to come to terms with the demands of critical appreciation and analysis of literature. Pupils were required to evolve their own learning strategy and working methods to handle the skills of character analysis, understanding of plot and theme, some consideration of imagery and close analysis of difficult textual passages. It was *not* intended that small-group talk would entirely replace other teaching methods, such as teacher instruction or lecturing, but that talk as a preliminary process would provide pupils with a fertile basis of understanding upon which other teaching methods would build more profitably. Pupils would receive and assimilate complex ideas more successfully if they had previously had the opportunity to explore and discover these ideas for themselves. There is a danger of over-estimating the ability of even able children to assimilate and fully understand comparatively simple ideas and information when they are presented to them by a teacher. Unfortunately, this situation is encouraged by the fact that pupils are often able to reproduce 'correct answers' in written form without ever fully understanding why they are correct.

The concern in this context, therefore, was not whether pupils could find the right answers by the use of talk, but whether they could develop the skills and strategies that would enable them to recognize and assimilate the right answer when it was offered. The teacher did not expect at this stage that the children would achieve great critical awareness, but it was intended that they should develop the skills of exploratory thinking to quite sophisticated levels.

Two major pieces of work were undertaken – the detailed study of *Macbeth* and the study of a number of examples of contemporary poetry. At this stage, the majority of pupils had some experience of small-group talk and they were made aware of the purpose of the use of talk by the teacher. A feedback session was held at the end of each term for the pupils to give their views on the successes and failures of the term's work. Tape-recorders were offered to any group that wished to use them for a session. The general pattern was that three or four groups would take recorders to areas outside the classroom and three or four groups would remain in the classroom.

i   *Macbeth*

The class was given a brief explanation of the nature of tragedy and an outline summary of the context and action of the play. They were then played a recording of the play, one act at a time, while they followed the text in their books. Groups were issued with a sheet of questions. The questions were carefully structured and required detailed reference to and study of the text of the play. Pupils were asked to analyse character by inference from the evidence presented in the text, to summarize plot and motive and to explain difficult textual passages. The questions were academic in nature and obviously placed considerable demands upon the pupils especially as they had little or no experience of this type of exercise. They were given no explanation of the questions but were asked to discuss fully each question in their groups until they were satisfied with their conclusions. They were told to write answers to the questions only after they had completed their talk.

Two girls, Mary and Ann, produced a tape of their talk which was quite remarkable. The talk itself lasted for forty minutes without interruption and throughout the girls approached the task with the utmost concentration and care. From the outset they adopted a particular method to handle the task systematically. One girl read the question and set up her own hypothesis as to its possible answer and solution. The other girl then considered this hypothesis, setting it against the evidence presented by the text and her own ideas and intuitions. From this situation they evolved, in most cases, a statement which was often an amalgam of both points of view and which they felt answered the question satisfactorily. They took great care not to proceed to another question until they were *both* happy with their conclusions on the previous question. During the talk, they alternated the two roles which were the basis of their methodology. If they could not come to a mutually agreed conclusion or if there were doubts about their own conclusion, they retained the problem in abeyance until they could either seek advice or later evidence came to their aid. In the following extract, they were discussing the significance of the witches' prediction that Macbeth would become Thane of Cawdor:

1 MARY (*Reading from text*) . . . and then 'all hail to thee Thane of Cawdor'/ now wasn't the Thane of Cawdor a rebel?

2 ANN I think Macbeth is going to become a rebel and king/so . . .

3 MARY No, no/he's/that's just the person he was/the ex-Thane of Cawdor/ it doesn't mean to say that Macbeth is going to be a rebel does it?

4 ANN It does/didn't it say something like/um/the Thane/um/the Thane of Cawdor was an outlaw or something and . . .

5 MARY Doesn't mean to say he was an outlaw.

6 ANN Yes he is/he's going to be a rebel/the Thane of Cawdor was a rebel and that's what Macbeth is going to be when he kills the king and becomes the king himself.

7 MARY Oh yes/of course/that's it.

8 ANN You see?

9 MARY Yes, that's it because he is already Thane of Glamis, later of Cawdor and later King of Scotland.

10 ANN Yes/mm/let me look at it/he's going to be Thane of Cawdor and the king.

11 MARY Yes/well/*like* the Thane of Cawdor.

12 ANN The?

13 MARY Yes/that's what they predict.

14 ANN I don't know.

15 MARY (*Reading*) 'All hail Macbeth, All hail to thee Thane of Cawdor.'

16 ANN I'm not sure/that could mean that he's going to be *like* him.

17 MARY No he's going to be it because someone said that/um/he will/I remember now someone speaking that.

18 ANN Oh yes/when he killed the rebel he got his title.

19 MARY Did he kill him?

20 ANN Mmm/I think so.

21 MARY The Thane of Cawdor/umm . . .

22 ANN Didn't Macbeth kill the Thane of Cawdor and then he got the title for himself?

23 MARY Maybe.
24 ANN Oh I don't know/I'm not *sure* anyway.
25 MARY No.

In this instance, Ann set up a hypothesis [2] based on inferences from the evidence Mary had presented [1] and Mary challenged Ann's hypothesis [3 and 5] which forced Ann to make her ideas clearer and relate them to evidence from the play. This she did in [6] – clearly articulating her point of view. Mary then accepted Ann's point and they ensured that it was clear to both of them. Ann checked Mary's understanding [8], and Mary offered confirmation by restating the evidence [9]. However, when Ann checked their conclusions [10], they discovered a problem – was Macbeth going to become Thane of Cawdor and did he kill the original Thane of Cawdor himself? The first problem they resolved by referring once again to the evidence referred to in the text. The second problem, however, they could not resolve satisfactorily.

What is important here is not whether they were right or wrong (although they did discover the irony in Macbeth becoming the Thane of Cawdor), it is the effectiveness of the learning process they were engaged in.

The problem with which the girls were concerned in this extract was not a major one in the play, but the strategies they adopted and the care they took with their task suggested that they would be capable of handling the more complex issues.

The following elements are apparent:

a the willingness to set up hypotheses for examination;

b the willingness to challenge stated hypotheses with positive and constructive criticism;

c the recognition of the need to articulate ideas clearly;

d the habitual reference to textual evidence to support ideas;

e the recognition of the necessity constantly to check and monitor their own performance.

In general, these elements are revealed in the girls' unwillingness to accept the quick and easy answer just to complete the task. Later they talked about the reasons for Macbeth being disturbed by the news that the king has made him Thane of Cawdor.

MARY Well how can the king be happy if he thinks that Macbeth is going to be the Thane of Cawdor/because the Thane of Cawdor was a rebel?
ANN No/look/I think it's when Macbeth killed/if he *did* kill the Thane of

Cawdor/he got his title/it doesn't mean that he's a rebel but he got his title.

MARY Yeah/that's what I was trying to say to you/but you said/oh/um/you know if he became/I said if he became the Thane of Cawdor/then you said if he became the Thane of Cawdor then he'd be a rebel or something/and you're just contradicting yourself.

ANN Um/no/what I meant by that is when the witches said it perhaps they meant it differently/perhaps they meant that he'd become *like* the Thane of Cawdor as well as having his title.

MARY Oh/I see what you mean.

ANN Any road/is that enough on that one?

Here again, Mary was quick to challenge Ann when she spotted a contradiction in her statement. It is important to note that this challenge was put in a very positive way, as the tape reveals. Rather than *accuse* Ann, it *invited* her to clarify her views. This Ann did – extending and developing her ideas. This extract also shows the girls' ability to retain for reference purposes their previous discussion – Mary spotted Ann's contradiction immediately and Ann was able to refer easily to the context of her earlier statement.

This same ability was revealed later when the teacher entered to discuss their progress with the girls:

1 TEACHER (*Entering room*) How are you getting on?

2 MARY All right thank you.

3 TEACHER Any problems?

4 ANN No not yet/not too many.

5 TEACHER How far have you got?

6 ANN Ummmm.

7 TEACHER You're just talking it through and not making notes?

8 ANN (*Anxiously*) No/we're not actually.

9 TEACHER It doesn't matter/I just wondered whether you've found that's the best way.

10 MARY Yes/well I can remember the answers now.

11 ANN Yes.

12 TEACHER You do?/OK/that's up to you/it depends on you individually/if you feel that between you this is an effective way to work then when you come to write you will be able to do it easily because you've talked about it beforehand.

13 ANN Yes/it seems umm/you/you sort of lose track if you're talking and writing at the same time/whereas/this way it comes smoothly.

14 TEACHER Yes/fair enough.

15 ANN Perhaps if the worst came to the worst we could borrow the tape again.

16 TEACHER Yes/sure/that's part of the reason for it.

17 MARY The thing is we don't know whether Macbeth killed the Thane of Cawdor/he didn't did he?

18 TEACHER No.

19 ANN He didn't?

20 TEACHER No/Macbeth was part of the King's forces against the rebels/he doesn't know at this stage when he meets the witches that the Thane of Cawdor was a rebel and had been captured/and this is the reason why he is so surprised when the witches tell him he will become the Thane of Cawdor.

21 MARY Why should they tell him that?

22 TEACHER Because they obviously have some knowledge of the future/they say 'Hail Thane of Glamis' which is his title anyway.

23 ANN AND MARY Yes.

24 TEACHER And the second thing they tell him is 'Hail Thane of Cawdor'.

25 MARY Why?/is it because he's going to get that title or is it because he's going to become a rebel like the Thane of Cawdor?

26 TEACHER Both/he is going to get that title and also, ironically, he's going to become a rebel as well.

27 MARY Oh I see.

28 ANN Yes I see.

The girls' responses to the teacher's inquiries as to their progress indicated the security they felt within the social and intellectual interaction provided by the talk situation. This was highlighted by Ann's comment [13] which indicated the success, by the girls' own standards, of the methods and strategies they had adopted.

Despite the fact that the original problem arose about fifteen minutes earlier, Mary was able to ask clear and precise questions [17, 21 and 25] which made it a very easy task for the teacher to offer help to clear up their misunderstanding. This, and other questions they asked, showed how easy it is for the teacher to teach, in the sense of passing on information and ideas, when the pupils have been through the initial exploratory and discovery stages themselves. Later in their discussion the girls managed to tackle and solve far more complex problems with little guidance from the teacher.

In the following example the girls discussed a question, quoted by Ann at the beginning, which required them to analyse, understand and draw inferences from a fairly complex speech by Lady Macbeth:

1 ANN 'What does Lady Macbeth consider to be Macbeth's weakness in Act 1, Scene 5?'/Oh/that was it/he didn't have enough ambition wasn't that it?

2 MARY Yes.

3 ANN Yeah/that's it/'he is too full of the milk of human kindness'/he is too soft.

4 MARY Well/yes/by her standards he was because/because he doesn't really want to hurt anybody/kill anybody to get his position/but she realizes this is impossible so she'd have to.

5 ANN Ummm/well he does/It's got *'not without* ambition but without the illness should attend it'/he's got ambition but not got the punch to further it.

6 MARY Yes/exactly.

7 ANN He's got it in him but he hasn't got the nerve to go on with it you know.

8 MARY Yeah/he has/but he doesn't want to kill people to do it/doesn't want to hurt anybody/to harm anybody/he's got 'the milk of human kindness'/ he doesn't want to harm people to get what he wants.

9 ANN Um/yes.

10 MARY And he knows that's what he'll have to do/he'll *have* to harm somebody/that's why he isn't going/that's why he isn't going to.

11 ANN Yes.

12 MARY That's about it then.

Ann started to analyse the question [1 and 3] by close reference to the text and offered a preliminary conclusion. But, significantly, the girls were not prepared merely to accept the first 'answer' that came along but proceeded to challenge and question their own assumptions. The result was that Mary [4] offered a qualification to Ann's original idea and Ann herself realized that her original hypothesis was inadequate [5 and 7]. She used evidence from the text to support the vital qualification she was making and, in order to confirm her own understanding, she translated the textual reference – 'not without ambition but without the illness should attend it' – into her own language – 'He's got ambition but not got the punch to further it.' The girls' ability to articulate their understanding in terms of their own language, which they demonstrated in this extract, is a very important part of their learning process and would appear to be encouraged and developed by small-group talk. In this example the girls managed to achieve a balanced and perceptive insight into the material they were studying.

Of course not all groups achieve this type of success. Most groups need constant monitoring, motivation and advice, especially in a task of this difficulty. Teacher intervention, as in the above example, is vitally important in order that pupils can make the most profitable use of talk sessions. The extract below from the tape produced by three girls from the same class, shows how groups can fail to achieve valuable learning experience from talk.

1 HEATHER Scene 1, Question 1/'Why do you think Shakespeare starts the play with the short witches scene?'
2 TANYA An introduction.
3 ANNA Yeah.
4 HEATHER Question 2.
(*Laughter*)
5 HEATHER No/creates atmosphere/got to do it properly.
6 TANYA Yes/and to know what's happening.
7 HEATHER Gives a brief outlook of what the play's going to be like.
8 TANYA Sort of like/umm/so you know what's going to happen in the future.
9 ANNA What's happening now/and what's going to happen.
10 HEATHER Insight (*laughs*) past present and future/right/Scene 2/ 'What's been happening in Scotland before the play?'
11 TANYA A war/it's a rebellion against the king isn't it?
12 HEATHER Yes/Question 3/'What information about Macbeth's character do we obtain from the scene?'
13 TANYA He's very courageous.
14 ANNA Hum . . .
15 HEATHER Question 4.
(*Laughter*)
16 TANYA Hang on hang on/we can't go too quick.
(*Laughter*)
17 HEATHER Well I mean we've answered the question.
18 TANYA Yeah/but how are we going to take notes from it?/just put one sentence answer/one word answer?/courageous/well he is very courageous/ (*laughs*)/what else did we say we were going to say?/didn't we say something else?

The comparison with Mary and Ann is obvious. The girls were happy to accept any answer that emerged, hypotheses, when they appeared, remained unchallenged and few ideas were developed in detail. Both Heather [5] and Tanya [16 and 18] showed awareness of their failure, but appeared to be unable to find any solution to the problem. Heather indicated the root cause of their failure when she said 'Well I mean we've answered the question' [17]. They were concerned not with the process of discovery and discussing solutions but with finding the 'correct answer'. This is oral comprehension in which talk is influenced by the demands of written exercises, something to which pupils are more accustomed.

The answer to this problem is practice and help. A great deal of time was spent with this group sitting in on their talk giving guidance and trying to increase their own confidence in a situation which they found difficult and often discouraging. The great advantage of small-group talk is that it does release the teacher to give his full attention to groups or individuals who experience difficulties. There are, of course, no set procedures or methods for encouraging group success in this type of activity. Much depends upon the nature of the relationship between teacher and class and between the individual members of a group, and the teacher must evolve a pragmatic and exploratory approach in dealing with groups who are experiencing difficulties. The teacher must be aware of the considerable power he possesses to guide, and even control, small-group activity and this power should be used with care and restraint. Ideally, the teacher should aim to become, if only temporarily, a natural member of the group he is visiting, participating in their talk so that any change of course he instigates appears to come organically from their talk and is not imposed by an 'outside authority'. If the teacher imposes a methodology on the group, he will endanger a vital part of the learning process that he hopes will be taking place.

ii Chips with Everything

In the previous example of teacher intervention, the purpose of the teacher's visit was to monitor group progress and to solve specific problems the group had discovered. In the following example, the teacher's intention was different: he attempted to change the course of the group talk in order to relate their discussion to their own experience. Based on their study of Chips with Everything by Arnold Wesker, three boys were discussing the merits of different political systems:

1 NIGEL Communism I think is the worst class structure there is/I mean you don't have any middle class/you either have the people in power or the people without power.
(Teacher enters)
2 JAMES Oh yes/but how about those who live in the Moscow flats/with television and jobs in/I don't know/Moscow or somewhere/those are the middle class in Russia.
3 NIGEL Yes/but/all that might be *material* benefit/but you have not got any freedom/and I think freedom is the most expensive commodity in the world.
4 KEVIN Yes/but that's being more equal than others isn't it?
5 NIGEL You can't buy freedom.
6 TEACHER You can't eat it either.

7 NIGEL No I suppose freedom from starvation and things like that are more important than just freedom.

8 TEACHER That comes first/but you can't stop there I suppose.

It can be seen that the teacher joined the group without disturbing their discussion in any way; they continued without hesitation. Yet when he made a comment [6], Nigel [7] very quickly backed down from his previous position as if bowing to the teacher's authority. The teacher then attempted to encourage Nigel by offering a comment which gave support to his previous ideas [8]. The situation in which the authority of the teacher would impose a restriction on the authority created by the group's free exchange of ideas was avoided. This shows that the teacher must remain constantly flexible, continually monitoring and reassessing his own contributions and their influence on the group. The discussion continued for a while until the teacher intervened again.

9 TEACHER There is a much bigger differential between low and high paid workers than there is in this country/there is a bigger incentive than in a capitalist country/it's not always in money as you said/they have a flat or priority on a car or they can go on holiday to the Black Sea instead of Siberia or somewhere/but bring it back to yourselves/you're in a top set/OK/would you be prepared to scrap this and go into a mixed-ability group?

10 KEVIN Oh no/I'd be slowed down by people who were less able than ...

11 NIGEL I don't agree with grammar schools though.

12 JAMES Oh I do.

13 NIGEL I mean you put an intelligent person when they're 11 years old into a grammar school.

(*Teacher leaves*)

14 NIGEL Deserter!

15 JAMES I don't think he agrees with grammar schools.

16 NIGEL How can you tell at 11 years old whether a person is going to be intelligent or not?

17 JAMES Because they pass their 11+.

18 KEVIN That doesn't prove anything/you are judged at 11/at 16 you take your O levels/your O levels will determine the rest of your life/so if you muck up your O levels you can muck up the rest of your life.

19 JAMES I could have not bothered about the first two years of this school/I didn't learn/what I learned in the first two years of this comprehensive school was minimal.

20 TEACHER (*From an adjoining room*) You are making an awful lot of noise out there.

(*Pause*)

21 JAMES That was Communism in action.

In this instance, the teacher considered that there was a danger that the discussion would flounder in an area too far beyond the group's own experience and he attempted to focus their attention on an issue very closely related to their own experience. He attempted to link this new direction to the previous discussion and, rather than impose a new subject, asked a related question, [9], which pointed towards this new area of discussion in the hope that the group would find and develop it for themselves. This was indeed what happened and the teacher was able to leave the group almost immediately, although branded as a 'deserter' by the group. This comment itself indicates that the teacher was regarded as a temporary member of the group rather than an outside authority.

The example above shows that the teacher's role in small-group talk is both very important and also very complex and he must learn with his pupils how to use and develop the opportunities it offers, especially when studying material of some complexity.

iii *Poetry*

During one term, the O-level group studied a number of poems by contemporary writers. These were often grouped thematically, two or three poems being studied in one session. The teacher read the poems to the class and the pupils were then asked to tackle a number of tasks together. The tasks were designed to be more flexible than those concerned with *Macbeth*. It was hoped that the pupils would develop the freedom to explore the poems in their own way and to relate the themes and subjects of the poetry to their own ideas and experience.

In practice, it was found that it was difficult to maintain the balance between tasks which gave the pupils such a tight structure, for example, in the form of a number of specific questions, that they had little freedom to explore their own ideas, and tasks which were so vague as to give pupils little security or material on which to base their talk.

A particular intention behind most of the tasks given to the pupils was to ensure that the discussion of their own ideas and experiences was conditional upon their previous, full understanding of the poems they had read. This was intended to avoid the situation in which literature is used purely for illustrative purposes and to encourage the further development of the skills of critical analysis and appreciation referred to earlier.

The material and task used met with varying success. The following extract is from the tape of four boys discussing the Roger McGough poem 'Let me Die a Youngman's Death' in which the poet says that, after a long life, he hopes to die the violent death of a young man rather than the peaceful 'out of breath death' of old age. The actual questions they considered are referred to in utterances [3] and [18].

1 JAMES 'Let me die a youngman's death'.
2 NIGEL I think that one is/I mean honestly/it's morbid isn't it?
3 JAMES 'What do you think the poet particularly fears about growing old?'
4 KEVIN Well if he gets older he's going to get all wrinkled and old and senile and . . .
5 JAMES And all the other things that are associated with old people.
6 KEVIN Generally talking about old things in the past that nobody else remembers/only him.
7 NIGEL When he goes he wants to be reported in the papers or something.
8 JAMES He doesn't want to be a nobody/he wants to be someone.
9 NIGEL He wants to be a hero.

In this section the group as a whole co-operated to construct a hypothesis together. The boys fed in evidence to construct a picture of the main character in the poem. Each contribution both restated a previous one and also supplied further ideas or information. Thus James' point [8] formed a generalization based on the interpretation offered by Nigel [7]. This mutual discovery and building process was a strategy used by the group in much of their work and it indicated the security of the social interaction that formed between them. This is different from the mere repetition of the point of view of others or the working to an easy consensus which some groups employ when they find progress difficult. Individuals monitor and evaluate group progress as they proceed and are prepared to challenge and question ideas or theories as they emerge. Thus, in the next section of the discussion, Kevin realized that they were on the wrong track and challenged Nigel's statement of the group idea [10] and produced evidence from the poem to support his challenge [12].

10 KEVIN I don't think he does.
(Pause)
11 JAMES No/he didn't because he says 'When I'm 73 and in constant good tumour.'
12 KEVIN He says 'not a famous-last-words death'/he doesn't want to be . . .
13 NIGEL Yes ⎫
14 DAVID Yes ⎬ (together)
15 KEVIN Yeah ⎭
16 KEVIN I mean he doesn't want to say 'I shall return' or . . .
17 NIGEL When they say it's their last words/how do they know it's their last words?

The above point was discussed for a few minutes. It can be seen that the group left the point they had been considering and followed Nigel's sudden tangential idea [17]. To a teacher this may seem to be a waste of time and a weakness in the group's handling of the task but it should be remembered that such diversions are a very natural part of talk. Adults often indulge themselves in sudden changes of subject, passages of humour and the like when they are in conversation and if we expect children to evolve a natural social interaction when they are talking in small groups we should expect to find the same features in their conversation. This should not be confused with idle chatter which is obviously counterproductive and the difference is shown by the manner in which the group returned easily and naturally to their given task:

18 JAMES 'To what extent do you sympathize with his point of view?'
19 KEVIN I don't.
20 JAMES I do.
21 KEVIN Why is that?
22 JAMES Poor kid wants to knock himself off when he's a little kid/well not a little kid but . . .
23 KEVIN He wants to die at 34 so that he'll always be young.
24 DAVID He doesn't want to be old.
25 NIGEL So he wants to . . .
26 JAMES Yes/but a young man is not 34.
27 NIGEL He doesn't want to die a young man/he just wants to die a young man's *death*/which means when he's old he dies a young man's death/what he thinks is a young man's death is being run down by a sports car after going to a party.
28 DAVID Yeah rather than being a doddering old man.
(*General agreement*)
29 KEVIN Discovered by his mistress in bed with her daughter – disgusting!
30 NIGEL Yes/yet another analogy springs to mind.
31 DAVID He wants to do something daring that he wouldn't normally do.
32 JAMES So when he says 'I'm 73 and . . .'/that's what he *wants* to happen to him?
33 NIGEL Yes.
34 DAVID Yes.
35 JAMES He wants to get run over by a red sports car.
36 NIGEL Well I doubt if he *wants*/well . . .
37 DAVID Yeah I know.
38 KEVIN He wants an almost violent death.
39 NIGEL Yes/not a 'nice way to go to death'/'*nice*'.
40 JAMES So it's that type of death he wanted/OK?

In this section the group once again built ideas together but, as before, individuals served a valuable function in challenging and directing progress. Kevin's question to James [21] forced him to give reasons for his opinion. The ability to give and take questions, however simple, is a vital part of the interaction of the group in successful discussion. If members of the group do not have the confidence to challenge the views of others or to ask them to elaborate on their stated ideas then the discussion as a whole will tend to be superficial and lacking in energy. Equally, individuals must be able to accept challenge and questions without rejecting them as personal attacks. James' reasons for his opinion led Nigel to challenge his ideas and identify a misconception in the group's hypothesis [27]. It is interesting that Nigel took great trouble here to articulate precisely his objection. He realized that the distinction he was making was a vital one in order that the group fully understand the poem and it was therefore important that he ensured that they received his message very clearly. The tape reveals that he made this statement with considerable force, placing appropriate emphasis to underline his point. This illustrates another useful function of small-group talk in that it forces individuals to find the appropriate language and style of expression to make their ideas clear, because there is an immediate audience who will challenge and question any lack of clarity or explicitness. In this instance Nigel's contribution enabled the group to modify and amend their ideas until they arrived at a satisfactory conclusion with James' final statement [40].

The poem the boys were studying was not a difficult one but it is open to misinterpretation. The teacher could obviously avoid this misinterpretation on the part of his pupils by giving them a few minutes direct instruction but this would deny them a valuable learning experience. The pupils were learning how to explore and handle the material they were given and to identify and correct their own errors and misconceptions. The strategies they were developing here would be equally applicable to material of far greater complexity. To answer the question 'What have they learned?', one should look as much at the *process* of their talk as at its product.

Towards the end of the term, groups were given tasks which were designed to test and develop their ability to handle difficult material with very little guidance either in the form of teacher instruction or specific questions which they were required to answer. They were provided with four complex poems on the subject of death and were asked to analyse the attitude towards death that each poem revealed. The teacher was interested to see if groups could evolve their own questions which would help them come to terms with the material. In a sense, he was trying to induce the groups to adopt a certain working strategy in which they would find it impossible to make a general statement about each poem and would be forced to break down the poem by setting up specific questions which analysed the components of its meaning. The danger was, of course, that they would be content with a vague generalization.

This is how Mary and Ann approached the poem 'An Irish Airman Foresees His Death' by W. B. Yeats.

1 MARY The next one I think is really good.
2 ANN 'An Irish Airman . . .'
3 MARY This must be the feeling of most Irish people.
4 ANN Not necessarily Irish people/because it's an old one/an airman in the First World War.
5 MARY Oh yes.
6 ANN Yes but I see what you mean/it's appropriate for the Irish people now.

(*They discuss the Irish situation, with particular reference to the acceptance of death as a natural and ever-present danger.*)

7 ANN Anyway/how about this poem/flying/it's such a danger.
8 MARY He's got a slight fear/but he's not really petrified.
9 ANN No, I think he feels/if it's to come it comes/you know/may as well take it/may as well accept it.
10 MARY Everyone in their life comes to realize what might be at the end of it.
11 ANN 'No likely end could bring them loss or leave them happier than before'/that's got something in it I think/'No likely end could bring them loss'/perhaps/he probably wouldn't be missed and then again they might not/umm/he might not be missed if he was killed.
12 MARY I think in the foreseeable future if death was the thing that was going to happen/it would not be worse than what was happening at that time.
13 ANN I don't get you/sorry.
14 MARY Nothing could be worse than the war so if death came it would not be worse than the fighting and the other deaths.
15 ANN Yes/just one in a million to be killed to go down/I think he is going to take death/and life/as it comes.
16 MARY It says second from the end 'A waste of breath the years behind'/ it's just a waste of time/it doesn't get anyone anywhere.
17 ANN Yes/that's true.

At the start of this example the girls revealed much hesitation – they were groping for an approach to the poem. To give themselves a start

Mary [3] suggested a parallel between the ideas expressed in the poem and the contemporary situation in Northern Ireland. Ann, at first, misinterpreted Mary's point [4], but when she realized what Mary meant [6] both girls explored the idea together. Thus, they achieved some common ground and formed a basis of understanding which enabled them to consider the poem in general terms. This was the first stage in the methodology they were evolving. This done, Ann then brought the discussion back to the poem itself [7] choosing a point at random in order to commence a more detailed analysis. Again, after discussing this issue, Ann narrowed the focus even further by introducing a quotation from the poem which had caught her attention [11]. This enabled the girls to identify the theme of the poem in more precise detail [12–15] and eventually Mary selected a final quotation [16] which supported the conclusions they had reached.

It can be seen that the girls evolved a very successful methodology. The strategy of progressively narrowing their perspectives of the poem enabled them to go beyond mere generalization to a detailed exploration of the poem's meaning.

With increasing experience, members of the O-level group were able to adapt themselves to a wide range of material of varying difficulty and complexity. Small-group talk became a natural part of their day-to-day work without necessarily being instigated by the teacher. Practice increased the sophistication and efficiency of their strategies and methods as they learnt how to handle the range of material they were offered. Much development of their critical faculties was required which indicated a point of great importance: the skills of exploratory thinking in small groups must be continually guided and encouraged for real progress to take place.

Conclusions

In this chapter we have covered only a small part of the work which was done with the O-level and CSE groups, and even that was only a component of the fourth-year syllabus. We started this work in an attempt to solve a problem we had identified within the workings of the English department. The results of the work would suggest that we had gone some of the way to finding a solution, and what we have tried to show is that talk as a learning process proved to be a valuable aid in furthering the pupils' enjoyment and understanding of literature.

This is not to suggest that small-group talk is a panacea, nor that it will always be successful. In fact, the use of talk in this way requires on the teacher's part a higher degree of organization and supervision than more traditional teaching methods. Careful structuring of tasks and monitoring of children's progress is essential if the teacher is not to abrogate his responsibility towards the children in his care. The success of group talk depends more upon the teacher–pupil relationship than do the more formal aspects of the teaching of English. Without an established working relationship between the teacher and pupil it is unlikely that groups of pupils themselves will form an effective working relationship. None the less, the effort to achieve such a secure working basis is well justified by the results that can be produced.

In our experience, the use of talk can be counter-productive if it is used so frequently that the children become bored with it and if the activity does not appear to be a natural part of normal classroom activity, but is set up artificially. Preferably talk should arise naturally out of the routine work of the class.

Constant monitoring and teacher intervention is necessary to give pupils adequate support and direction in order that they may fully exploit their responses and intuitions about literature. This intervention can take many forms. The teacher may merely check on a group's progress and answer any immediate questions relating to the work. In other situations, particularly in cases in which groups appear to be making little progress, he may join in the discussion to give the group guidance and impetus. The most important factor in all these situations is that the teacher should not use his authority to take over and dominate group activity. Often more can be achieved to assist a group by the use of carefully chosen questions than by direct instruction.

The use of talk would appear to be compatible with the specific demands of public examinations. Despite the time consumed in the short term by talk, it may well provide the basis on which pupils may arrive at a deeper and fuller understanding of texts studied than can be achieved by other methods.

Talk is not a substitute for other activities but is a means of facilitating the learning process and an effective method of helping pupils come to terms with and extend their understanding of 'adult literature' and the period of change called adolescence. James Britton sums up the importance to the adolescent of talk in *Language and Learning*: *

---

* See James Britton, *Language and Learning* (Allen Lane, Penguin Press, 1971), p. 223.

Perhaps the most important general implication for teaching . . . is to note that anyone who succeeded in outlawing talk in the classroom would have outlawed life for the adolescent; the web of human relations must be spun in school as well as out.

III. Talking and writing

Neither form of language [talking or writing] at secondary level can be used for long to the exclusion of the other; indeed our view would be that many learning situations could often be improved if the two were more closely interrelated.

Writing and Learning across the Curriculum 11–16
(Ward Lock Educational, 1976)

There is a common assumption, often shared by teachers and pupils, that talking and writing are totally separate activities, and, moreover, that writing is work and talking is recreational. How many teachers have been asked, 'Do we have to work? Can't we have a discussion instead?'

The logical extension of this attitude, namely that talking is time-wasting, is a good example of a self-fulfilling prophecy. The teacher assumes that talking is unprofitable, rightly stamps on it, and the idea of talk as a non-valuable, and therefore undesirable, activity is reinforced. Henceforth, the talk in the classroom is unlikely to have any educational value.

The really unfortunate feature of this attitude is that it blinds teachers to the possibilities of using talk to assist learning, not least in helping the written work. The positive feature to be discovered is that talk, which is regarded by the pupils as not work, can, therefore, be enthusiastically tackled and can produce improved written results: profit from pleasure.

We must now ask which 'learning situations could often be improved if the two [talking and writing] were more closely interrelated'.

In some learning situations pupils are seeking a single correct answer and here, perhaps, there is 'nothing to discuss', although that is, in itself, a debatable point. Frequently, however, pupils are dealing with very complex questions where there is no single 'right answer', and where the processes and means of achieving a solution may be as important as the solution itself. It is in these circumstances that talk may be especially valuable. Talk can help to make explicit the ways in which we reach the solutions of difficult problems, and enable us to build more readily on past experience. If we regard the written task as being a difficult problem, as indeed it is, we can see a single justification in the use of talk in connection with writing.

We should, then, be looking for talk to be of positive assistance in accomplishing written tasks and, for the sake of simplicity, we have concentrated on two areas: the sharing of ideas and the testing of ideas.

When dealing with complex situations where there is no single answer, no one has a monopoly on the truth and the nearest anyone can get to a 'right answer' is to form an amalgam of a number of people's insights, and the best way (indeed, in realistic school terms, the only way) of bringing these insights together for the benefit of all is by talking about them. Talk may be a valuable way of sharing ideas before they are committed to paper.

In the minds of most school pupils a piece of written work is usually a finished product, and even if asked to rewrite it most will produce a piece strikingly similar to the original. Yet all teachers know the value of reviewing work and trying out ideas in a rough form before producing the final product. Talking about a piece of written work before putting pen to paper, or even during writing, enables pupils to test out their ideas for accuracy, for general acceptance and for credibility before they attain that feeling of finality by being written. Talk can be used as a form of rough draft.

A piece of written work which is based on the shared ideas of a group of people, and which is in effect the final draft after extensive reworking, must at least stand a good chance of being superior to the first and final draft of one isolated mind. Talk offers possibilities of co-operative working which can lead to superior individual written work.

Examples of these processes in action are examined below. In the first, the emphasis is on the sharing of ideas, and in the second, on testing out ideas before producing a final draft. Obviously there is considerable overlap between the two.

1 Sharing and testing ideas through role-play

A fifth-year class was given an exercise, 'The Fight', based on the following notes.

THE FIGHT
On this sheet you will find an account of a fight in a school and its consequences. Assume that this is what actually took place and base your answers to the questions on it.

The true story
John Tough has a pen which he found but neglected to hand in. This pen belongs to Paul Strong who is in the same year as John. Paul sees John with the pen, tells John that it belongs to him and asks for it back. John refuses.

Paul tries to grab the pen. John then says, 'OK, if you want it I'll let you have it,' and flicks ink over Paul.

Paul then attacks John who drops the pen and fights back. During the fight Paul's head hits the wall, and one of his teeth is knocked out, while John's jacket is badly torn.

After a couple of minutes Jeff, a friend of John who has been watching the fight with Paul's friend Peter, decides that it is getting too serious and tries to pull them apart. Peter thinks Jeff is siding with John, and he joins in to help Paul.

At this point Mr Vain, a teacher, breaks up the fight, taking the names of all the boys involved.

The next day Mr Beaver, the Headmaster, has letters of complaint from Mr Tough and Mr Strong. Mr Beaver sends for John, Paul, Jeff and Peter, talking to each individually.

After meeting them he punishes the boys he thinks were wrong and replies to Mr Tough and Mr Strong.

Now do one task from each section
Section A   Tell the story of the fight in the words of either (*a*) John and Paul or (*b*) Jeff and Peter, making out as favourable a case as possible for each boy.

Section B   Write, in the correct form and style, the letters from either (*a*) Mr Tough to Mr Beaver, and his reply or (*b*) Mr Strong to Mr Beaver, and his reply.

Section C   Who do you think Mr Beaver will find is in the wrong? Be sure to give reasons for your answer.

It will be seen that the tasks set involved the use of a number of skills, the primary being the ability to produce a personalized and subjective account of events from an impersonal and objective account.

Before beginning the written tasks, one group of boys asked if they could use the exercise as a basis for role-play with each member of the group taking on one of the characters from the sheet. The group took a tape-recorder into a corridor and remained there until the end of the session brought an end to the talk.

The role-play went on for over half an hour: a remarkable span of concentration from an unsupervised group. What is even more remarkable is that the identification of the group with the characters survived a number of interruptions, including one from a teacher who commented on their noisy enthusiasm (a problem with having to do oral work in corridors which the group took without comment!).

The discussion was continuous and heated, and showed a remarkable ability on the part of the boys to take on the role of a character and retain identification. The following is an extract from an improvised conversation between the fictitious characters in the exercise.

1 PAUL Look, sir, it was his fault and that's that, sir.

2 PETER It was John's fault.

3 JOHN It wasn't, sir/I just found the pen, and I just thought/you know/I just thought it was one I had lost and then he comes up to me and . . .

4 PETER You should have handed it in/you knew it was his pen all along.

5 JOHN I just thought it was one I lost.

6 MR BEAVER Who started the fight, then?/who started the fight?

7 JOHN He did/he grabbed me.

8 PAUL He did/it's just 'cos he hates me, that's all.

9 JOHN It's not, sir/that's a lie.

10 PAUL He's always picking on me.

11 JOHN I ain't.

12 PAUL He ain't.

It will be seen that in this initial period of discussion there was much simple accusation and contradiction, the participants using all the available points one after the other with very little development. However, as the discussion progressed ideas were developed and new lines of argument introduced at regular intervals.

13 JOHN He started it, sir/'cos he just walked up to me and grabbed my pen.

14 PETER Mr Beaver, sir/it was his fault/I saw everything.

15 MR BEAVER Did you?

16 PETER (*Acting as witness for Paul*) Yeah/I saw the fight/I saw his tooth get knocked out/I saw the ink get flicked all over him.

17 JOHN (*Realizing he needs a supporting witness himself*) Come on Jeff/Jeff, who started it?

18 JEFF (*Obliging*) He started it/he came up and took the pen.

19 PAUL Oh, come on, sir!

20 PETER (*Again leaping in to help Paul*) Look at the state of this kid's mouth.

21 PAUL Yeah, look at me.

22 JOHN (*Not to be beaten*) He never asked him for his pen/he just came up and tried to take it.

23 PAUL (*Sensing he has to attack*) Then he flicked ink all over my face, he did.

24 JOHN (*Developing Jeff's point*) It was an accident, and then he started attacking me.

25 PETER (*Going back to the duplicated sheet for support*) You goes, 'if you want your pen back then, Paul, here's the ink'/flick!/all over his face.

26 PAUL (*Backing up Peter*) That's what he said.

27 JEFF He tried to snatch it.

28 PAUL (*Continuing his argument regardless*) Look at it all over me face/he did it on purpose.

29 JEFF (*Persevering*) He tried to snatch the pen/you liar.

30 JOHN (*Pressing home Jeff's advantage*) Well, you shouldn't attack me.

31 PETER (*Leaping to support Paul*) He tried to snatch the pen back because it was his in the first place, which he nicked off him.

32 JOHN (*Having to deal with this most serious charge*) I didn't nick it/I found it.

This extract demonstrates the considerable change which occurred in the quality of the talk and the level of argument. Sophisticated techniques were being employed: stances were changed when they became insupportable; advantages were followed up. More striking, perhaps, is the way that one character supported another, both building on the other's points. Some really effective arguments were used, and it is obvious that there was considerable identification between the boys and the characters they were playing: 'Look at the state of this kid's mouth' [20]; 'Look at it all over me face' [28].

It may have been noticed that the basic position being adopted by John and Paul on such issues as the ownership of the pen, who started the fight and so on, had been changing. In the first extract, for example, John said, 'I just thought it [the pen] was one I lost' [5], while in the second extract he said (as a reaction to the serious charge of having stolen the pen), 'I didn't nick it. I found it' [32]. No mention at the later stage of thinking it was his; that would have been too dangerous. The ability of the boys to adapt to changing circumstances is a characteristic of the first part of the discussion.

Perhaps this changing of positions led to some confusion in their minds but the boys decided that it was necessary to state clearly their new positions, so first Paul and then John gave a run-down of their revised stories. From these it became clear that each had recognized weaknesses in his initial position and abandoned them, but had also detected the other's weaknesses and exploited them.

Later on in the improvisation, the fictitious character Paul found it unnecessary to accuse John of theft: 'He started making all this fuss that he didn't know it was mine,' and made his strongest point about the ink-squirting; then he started saying, 'All right, if you want your pen back, here it is,' and 'He flicked ink in my face.'

John, on the other hand, no longer claimed that the pen was his, and admitted to using a pen that he had found: 'I thought it was just some pen that somebody had lost, and I was using it in class', but in return made a great play of the accusation that Paul had started the fight: 'This twit came up to me and grabbed it.' He also had an excuse for the ink-squirting incident: 'When he grabbed it all this ink . . . sort of went and squirted everywhere.'

The role-play continued after this in the same vein, with new points being brought in, and with a considerable contribution from Peter and Jeff, so that the four were put on a roughly equal basis in terms of their part in the discussion.

At the end of the lesson the boys in the group went away to tackle the written tasks. In Section A they were asked to 'Tell the story of the fight in the words of either (a) John and Paul or (b) Jeff and Peter, making out as favourable a case as possible for each boy.' This allowed scope for the pupils to write as if they were speaking, and the role-play could be directly applied here. At the same time it demanded that the pupils write an uninterrupted statement of events from the point of view of one of the characters in the role-play, whereas, in the role-play the constant interruption of argument meant that such an ordered presentation was not possible. So the task demanded more than just writing out part of what was said.

The results of the written work were very interesting. The following is what the boy who played John wrote in response to the dramatic experience of the improvisation:

John's story
I found this pen you see in my class and so I picked it up, not realizing whose it was and plus my pen was running out of ink. Anyway, I decided to borrow it for a couple of days.

Anyway I was sitting down in the classroom when there was this tug on the back of my jacket and I could feel a rip right down my sleeve. Turning around I saw Paul there accusing me of stealing his pen; trying to explain to him about the situation he just wouldn't listen to me and started to shout even louder, and then he came across and started tugging. I was just about to give in and give him the pen when all the ink came out and spurted in his face.

Trying to apologize to him, in which I couldn't succeed, he came over and thumped me really hard at which I staggered back. Not wanting to have a fight I walked away but again he came over and hit me. Not standing for that I began to thump him back, not really hard, but I lost my temper. That's when he ripped all of my jacket. At this I hit him once more and he hit his head on the wall. It was just an accident and I felt bad. I stopped at this and went across to see if he was all right. Then the next thing I knew his friend, Peter, was coming up to me and starting to punch me. Then I noticed that Paul had got up and was also starting to beat me up. Then my friend Jeff came in to break it up, but they just wouldn't have that, so they carried on fighting and that's where you came in, sir.

This account, though it may be stylistically imperfect, has many encouraging features. It is abundant in small details – the location of the fight, the attempt by John to discuss the situation and apologize to Paul – which add verity to the story, and have the desired effect of making John far less to blame than the original 'true account' suggests. So the writing emerged as a strong defence of John, one which had obviously resulted from the role-play and which showed the sophistication which the talk had attained.

This writing may be compared with that produced by a girl of similar ability who had not taken part in the role-play, approaching the task 'cold'.

John's story
I found a pen and meant to hand it in but what with one thing and another I forgot. Then yesterday Paul came up to me and accused me of pinching his pen. Well, I didn't know if it was his or not, did I? So I didn't say anything but he then tried to grab it off me and the fight started during which Paul hit his head and my jacket got torn.

Although this piece may be superior in terms of written style, in every other way it is inferior: it is briefer than the original stimulus material, is less detailed and alters little. The only concession to the fact that this is supposed to be John's version is the omission of the ink-throwing incident. There is no attempt to counter points that Paul would undoubtedly raise, nor does John use those points, such as his torn jacket, which count in his favour. All in all, the piece lacks interest, detail and an appreciation of the type of writing required.

There may be many reasons why there were such marked differences between the two pieces of writing, although the fact that the work of those who took part in the role-play was consistently better than that of the others, as well as being better than their normal standard, makes it not unreasonable to suggest that, since many of the ideas and stratagems used in the discussion were included in the writing in modified form, the talk had at least given the participants some new ideas and an appreciation of the points of view of others.

2 Sharing ideas and using talk in a co-operative effort

In the previous example we were looking at the way in which talk may assist writing by giving pupils opportunities to share ideas and test out their schemes before writing and thus produce written work with fewer ill-considered ideas. Talk can also be employed during the process of writing as a means of checking on the progress of work in hand: a means whereby what has been done may be reviewed, and either confirmed or rejected.

A group of third-year boys, in the process of reading *My Side of the Mountain* by Jean George, were asked to produce a brochure which was to be designed as an aid to the survival of someone lost or stranded in wild country. Each member of the group had taken a section or sections and worked on them individually.

The result of the work was very impressive: a large folder with sections on wild plants, fungi, birds' eggs, fire-lighting, trapping, etc. It was obvious that a lot of effort had been put into these individual sections, as well as a great deal of thought. Having mustered the individual contributions, the group put them into a folder and handed in this 'finished' product.

While the sections themselves were excellent in isolation, the brochure as a whole lacked structure and organization, and was not ideally suited for the purpose for which it was intended, that is, as an aid to survival.

The teacher at this point had a number of choices: he could have left the brochure as it was, applauding the individual contributions; he could have instructed the group on how to reorganize the brochure into a more useful form; or he could have made a preliminary suggestion, and then left the group to talk about the problem and let them reach their own solution. In fact, this last course was employed.

The teacher began by praising the work already done and outlined what he saw as the problem:

> TEACHER What you've got so far is you've got very nice sections/but what I think you want to talk about now is how you organize it into being a really good survival guide/I don't think it's as useful as a survival guide as it might be, because at this moment it's almost a list of things you need/a few

tips/you see this survival guide here/there's a tremendous amount of writing in it to explain how to use things/how do you survive in the wild/I wonder whether you might like to try to discuss what you can do to make it a more useful guide.

With this and a few suggestions, such as considering the inclusion of an index and the need for linking the sections, the group was left to come to its own decisions on how to organize the brochure. They were being invited, in effect, to review the work they had already done, and then to co-operate in deciding how it should be altered or added to; in other words, to be an editorial committee.

At first the suggestions put forward were very simple, and pointed to the idea that the group had not thought much about the ordering of the material, and therefore was a bit lost:

SIMON What are we going to do?
ALAN Put them in alphabetical order or something.
ADRIAN Building, shelter, etc.
WILLIAM I mean it sounds . . .
SIMON We want to reorganize it.
ALAN Right/chuck out the index/new index.
SIMON What shall we put first?
ALAN Introduction/introduction.
DAVID No/index first.
WILLIAM Yes/index.
ALAN No/introduction first.
WILLIAM We've got an introduction.

At first sight this may seem a rather pointless conversation, but this sort of preparatory talk is all part of learning and is valuable.

A bit later a far more thoughtful idea was put forward when David, objecting to a suggestion of using alphabetical order, suggested putting the most important things first. This idea, so obviously sensible, was accepted without dissent, and a decision was quickly made to sacrifice the individual identity of the separate projects in order to bring about the suggested organization; thus birds' eggs, berries and fungi all went into the new section on food.

At this point, however, a dispute arose about which were the most important things. Even the idea of putting the most important things first seemed to get lost.

But then:

DAVID Hang on a minute, lads/listen a minute then/wouldn't you think/shh!/ shut up a minute/Peter, wouldn't you think it would be best to put the easiest food to find first, fungi and berries?

At last a point was made on the basis of logic: put the easiest food to find first. This immediately changed the whole course of the discussion; there was a need to answer logic with logic:

ALAN You're not going to go into the forest and start eating.
DAVID Well/you will if you're hungry.
GRANT You'd go into the forest and start to make a shelter to stay the night and then make a fire and find something to eat.

By this stage the group was doing what it was asked to do originally: to make the guide useful to a person who would really need it – someone lost in a wilderness. They were thinking of the priorities of someone in these circumstances. The discussion really came to life at that point and became very practical. Soon it was established that the order would be: shelter, fire, easy food; and that the easy food section would include berries, fungi, and birds' eggs. Once a basis of reason had been established decisions were made on all sides, and real progress achieved.

The next dispute arose about the positioning of trapping, and again the solution came from thinking about the practical situation:

WILLIAM What about trapping them first, before all that.
DAVID You only trap certain animals first day/the first day you get there you don't trap animals, do you?/right then.

There was a dispute about the place of fishing and this time the argument arose from projecting themselves through their imagination into the actual situation:

DAVID You just say you've done all that/you've gone to bed.
WILLIAM (*Obviously not impressed as yet*) Why fishing?/fishing isn't important.
ALAN (*Undeterred*) You wake up/you wake up/perhaps you have a few berries/ then you think of something to do/right, what do you do?
DAVID Get some berries.
WILLIAM (*Still not impressed and in sarcastic tone*) Yes/they really fill you up/ don't they?
ALAN (*Still undeterred*) What are you gonna need?
DAVID Fish.
GRANT Fish.
SIMON Fishing.
WILLIAM (*Beaten*) Fish.

The discussion went on for a few more minutes, sorting out other disagreements in a similar fashion.

It was a long discussion containing many disagreements, resulting from the need to reach a consensus. Although much of this may seem to be unproductive, the talk is a fine example of co-operative learning, whereby pupils came to terms with the problem in their own minds and in their own time, thereby both reaching a solution and finding out how solutions may be realized. To achieve this requires considerable patience on the part of the teacher.

The end-result of this heated discussion?

SURVIVAL: AN ILLUSTRATED GUIDE

Contents
As you can see in this survival guide we have put certain subjects into what we think are appropriate chapters.

Chapter 1   Shelter
Chapter 2   Fire
Chapter 3   Easy Foods to Find
Chapter 4   Fishing and Trapping
Chapter 5   Clothing
Chapter 6   Herbal, Medical and Poisonous Plants
Chapter 7   Equipment to Make

We have devised a survival guide which we hope will help anybody who is lost, boat capsized, etc.

Survival today is a menial task, with our highly developed world. But what is to happen when you are left alone to fend for yourself? Can you survive? What about warmth, food and somewhere to sleep?

That's where we come in. We hope to give you 'the urge' to go and live for a week, a month or even a year, alone, unaided, trying to live a healthy life, living on berries, mushrooms, the odd rabbit and maybe the odd bird's egg for Christmas! Still not interested? Well, what about the fun of building your own hut then, or even a tree house? Going fishing early morning?

It's up to you. Browse through this book, finding things of interest from tits to edible fungi. Anyway, read and enjoy, we hope!

The final order was highly logical, and much thought had obviously gone into making the introduction suitable for the whole brochure. For those who might find this introduction too whimsical, there was an introduction to each chapter which showed the serious side of the brochure.

Chapter 1: Shelter
In this chapter we describe how to make a shelter, be it made of branches, or of tree trunks or of stones.

It shows diagrams of these different sorts of huts as well as writing to go with it.

This chapter introduction is simple and to the point, wholly suited to the subject-matter of the chapter, and of the guide overall.

It would seem that the discussion had contributed to the production of a highly satisfactory end-product, for the brochure was a very competent piece of work in its final form, as well as being a co-operative effort, as the introduction proves. The guide had form, structure, an internal logic to its organization, and included some additional material which the reorganization made necessary.

Once encouraged, the group revised the shape and form of their first effort and decided on improvements which they could make. The process took longer than it would have done if the teacher had given the group specific instructions. The group reasoned-out an answer for themselves, survived distractions and learned a lot about methods of working along the way. Teachers, concerned as they often are about what people will think of them, tend to be too impatient to allow this co-operative process to progress to a conclusion: they halt it half-way through, maybe just before a crucial moment of progress, and thus write off the whole as a waste of time. In this case, the process was completed, and the benefits can be seen. The brochures produced by other groups who did not, for one reason or another, get a chance to review their efforts, showed the problems of this group's initial product. They tended to lack structure, consisted of obviously individual contributions, lacked linking material, failed to cater for any audience and omitted index and introduction.

The talk, it seemed, resulted in an improved written product. Perhaps the same result could have come from specific teacher instructions, but this would not have given the group the valuable experience of co-operative working or of joint decision-making.

3 Talk as a preparation for written work: instilling a sense of audience

The preceding two examples seek to illustrate the place of talk in improving the qualities of written work. They concentrated on two main areas: sharing ideas and thereby permitting a more considered piece of writing, and redrafting an original idea through discussion. There are other ways in which talk can be used in association with written work.

One of the problems which pupils often face in the classroom, although they may not acknowledge it consciously, is a failure to imagine the audience for whom they are writing. This is usually the responsibility of the teacher who is often the only person who reads the work, and it is he who suffers in the end, for work with no audience tends to lack interest and organization. It is difficult to persuade pupils that they are learning the indispensable skills of communication unless they are made aware of those at the receiving end of their work: their audience.

A simple, but effective means of giving pupils an idea of their relation to the audience is by employing group talk prior to writing. Having this sense of audience can help to make the written work more lively, interesting and organized as the pupils can gauge what others will accept and understand.

With this end in view, a group of third-year pupils were put into groups after reading a short story about a boy's relationship with his grandfather, and instructed to describe to each other as vividly as possible one of their grandparents. Having done this they produced a rough draft of their descriptions for homework. In the next lesson they read the drafts to the other members of the group, talked about how they might improve them and made a final copy.

Here the sense of audience was emphasized by the two discussion sessions; it soon emerged from them that the group was little interested in some aspects of their grandparents, and these were soon dropped. Other topics gained the whole attention of the group and were therefore pursued. With this help in subject-matter the first draft was made, with the second discussion session providing a chance to see whether their expression and organization were suitable.

If groups can get an idea of their audience there is more motivation to produce interesting and well-thought-out work, and group discussion can provide the sense of audience.

Conclusion

The evidence of this chapter seems to illustrate that talking can, and indeed does, enhance the quality of written work done by a class: it can help children to imagine more clearly the characters they are making up in narrative writing; and it can give them a sense of purpose both in relation to one another as members of a group, and also in relation to a potential audience beyond their own group.

IV. Differences between small-group talk and large-group talk

This chapter is an account of some of the differences noticed between the oral work done in small groups and oral work done with the class working together as a 'large group'.

The oral work from which this account stems was based on the study of novels, short stories and poems. The classes taped doing this work were two fourth-year groups, one potentially O level, the other potentially CSE. The small groups they used were of their own choosing, friendship groups of between three and six, which could be formed easily with the minimum of moving round the classroom, often by just turning round a few chairs. The class discussions were done with the whole of the form, thirty-six in the case of the O-level group, and twenty-two in the case of the CSE group. These class discussions were initially chaired by the teacher with the class facing each other round the room, but a slightly different arrangement was later tried in which, though the class sat round the room facing each other, the chairmanship was handed over to one of the pupils while the teacher sat outside the circle in a corner taking notes for the purpose of interpreting the tape-recording later on, and interrupting the class as little as possible. The value of this method was that it removed the teacher's influence from the discussion (something considered later in this chapter) and made it easier for the teacher to observe objectively what was happening. This last point is a very important feature of this method because the teacher seldom has the opportunity to study discussion closely while it is happening unless he goes into another teacher's lesson. Of course he may listen to a discussion on tape afterwards but tape-recorders do not always pick up the information, some of it visual, that is needed to interpret the events. Also, if the teacher leads the discussion or gives continual guidance it does make it harder to make objective judgements about what is happening; however, occasional comments or guidance from him may be needed.

The differences between large and small groups centre round the change in numbers and the presence of a different kind of audience. Surrounded by a small number of friends, a shy, quiet person can find the encourage-

84

ment to join in a discussion and it is easy to understand the remark of a girl who, writing about her experience of both class and small-group discussion, said, 'We speak more freely in smaller groups, especially with friends, as we do not get so embarrassed.' Surrounded by a larger number of people with whom one's relationship is uncertain and thus more formal, the situation can seem more threatening and, to use another pupil's comment, 'People do not like to give their viewpoints for fear of being laughed at or shouted at.' In the small friendship group lies the support of people you know, or (when it appears) a kind of aggression that is often easy to take since it comes from those you know. So there appears a perhaps somewhat crude, but basically sound, distinction between the small friendship group which is informal and socially easy and the class which is more formal and more threatening. Of course there are always exceptions: there are small groups who spend most of their time establishing a pecking order and being anything but socially easy; likewise there is the occasional person who finds that the stress of the class discussion is positively stimulating.

As well as characterizing the social nature of the groups it is possible also to characterize the type of comment to which grouping can lead. The following example may help to illustrate this point. A group of three boys from a fourth-year class was looking at the poem 'Not Waving but Drowning' by Stevie Smith and trying to sort out the different voices in it.

DONALD And so they/but one's still drowning and the other one's laying on the beach.
ADRIAN No/(*pause*)/oh if he was on the beach he would have tried to help his mate wouldn't he?
DONALD No he's not/he says it's laying moaning.
NEIL He probably swam out so far and thought oh my God I can't get back.
DONALD Maybe there's two/there's only two because he'd be going out and helping him if he/if he was ummm/if he lay moaning.
NEIL I reckon there's three.

Uncertain of the poem, they asked questions and suggested possible answers about how many people are there. The questioning, tentative groping for meaning and considering possibilities, is typical of the sort of discussion encouraged by a small friendship group.

By comparison, the class discussion is often a more threatening occasion during which there seem to be fewer examples of thinking out loud. The need to maintain a relatively stronger position, the fear of being criticized or questioned unexpectedly, leaves less room for voicing uncertainty. Pupils make statements which assume a less sympathetic audience and therefore tend to be more explicit, more firmly based on evidence, possibly showing a stronger sense of personal commitment to the view being put forward. Take, for example, the following extract from a class discussion, chaired by a pupil, which took place immediately after the class had finished reading *The War of the Worlds* by H. G. Wells. Thomas was referring back to a previous comment of Susan's about a central character and disagreed with it.

> THOMAS Susan said that/ummm/it was a bit boring the fact that it was him going all the way through you know and how he kept on missing everything.
>
> MATTHEW Superman! (*laughter from some*)
>
> THOMAS Like the heat ray/there were hundreds like him but *he* was the one who wrote the story/hundreds of people survived like him/(*incomprehensible mutter from others*)/but the others didn't write and he wrote the story about himself.

Despite interruptions Thomas made his point clearly, stating the case against which he wished to argue and then making his point in two separate ways. His statement was certainly explicit and though he did not give what one would call evidence to support his point he used a sophisticated method to impress his audience, restating Susan's point clearly before he confidently knocked it down.

These extracts from tapes are clearly not directly comparable: one shows a discussion where the meaning of lines is uncertain; the other shows critical comment on a book where the meaning is not in question. But they do suggest the difference in tone likely to be found in the two situations.

Another aspect of the difference between these situations is the degree to which the discussion is explicitly ordered, directed and defined. In the small group there is less of this than in the large group; among friends the rules are understood and seldom need stating, the direction of talk is easier to control since fewer people are taking part, and there is more likely to be a mutual understanding of the kind of talk which they are using. In the larger group the opposite is the case; for example, the comment that Thomas made in *The War of the Worlds* discussion above began with a clear statement that placed his contribution firmly in the mainstream of the discussion, showing its relevance by linking it back to a previous point. Later in the same discussion Luke followed exactly the same pattern.

> LUKE Those girls over there were complaining about all the description but if you were reading that book normally/you know not/not in class/you'd read the first chapter/say there's too much description for me and give it in.

Later still, another member of the group also prefaced her remarks with 'On the point he said about people believing that there are men on Mars, they didn't.' In the small group the individual's channel of thought obviously makes a more significant contribution to the mainstream so when he voices an idea it is more likely to seem relevant; smaller numbers mean that he can react more spontaneously. In the large group his channel of thought has less influence, he can speak less often and so the relevance of his comment has to be made explicit rather than being accepted.

With so many different channels of ideas feeding into the mainstream of the discussion not just the individual speaker but also the chairman sometimes needs to indicate which part of the mainstream is at that moment relevant. In a pupil-chaired class discussion about 'Not Waving but Drowning' the chairman, Alan, had already heard a number of different interpretations of the poem – some, explanations of individual lines, others, comments on the whole poem – and he saw a good opportunity to focus attention on to one of the most important areas.

ALAN Does anyone feel that *is* something to do with physically drowning?

This is the sort of explicit question that can be left out of the small-group discussion. In fact, a tape-recording of a group of five boys, including Alan, discussing precisely the same problem, shows that there seemed to be no need to indicate specifically what had to be looked at next because all the members of the group were contributing frequently to the discussion.

Another aspect of this explicit ordering, directing and defining of the class discussion can be seen in the way the chairman, or sometimes an individual, feels the need to keep the discussion going if it looks like flagging. For example, a point has been made in a class discussion, there are mutterings but no clear response and after a few moments the pupil chairman says hopefully, 'Comments on that point?' This feeling that things are going wrong if people are not talking seems to stem from a sense of the formality of the discussion; it would not feel right if there were long silences. Neither would it feel right to drift into the kind of chat that can easily occur in small-group work as it did in the case of the following small group of girls who were meant to be discussing a story by William Faulkner.

CHARLOTTE Did you see that film on Saturday night?
SUSANNE *Villain?*/oh isn't he beautiful/ah Richard Burton!
CHARLOTTE I'd rather have Paul Newman myself.

Again, the class discussion has more explicit and more limiting rules.

A further aspect of this can be seen in the way that the chairman of the class discussion has to control the number of speakers, choosing who speaks if there are too many who want to speak at once. In a class discussion about a poem a number of separate suggestions were made about the meanings: the girl chairing the group shouted 'Oi!' and a moment later when something like quiet had taken over, she asked, 'What was you gonna say, Nick?' In the small group less competition for the opportunity to speak makes such promptings less necessary.

In the large group the pupils are more likely to be aware of fixed and formal rules about the talk in which they are engaged and this awareness, this opportunity to think about the talk, must be a very useful stage in understanding its possible value. Talk is so often regarded as an easy and less important part of the work done in the classroom that anything which encourages an understanding of its possible usefulness must be good.

However, it would be wrong to assume that class discussions are broadly comparable to small-group discussions, but merely a little more formal; in many cases teachers know that there are big differences between them, differences which can give class discussion considerable disadvantages. Three of the more obvious ones are these: there is a proportionately small number of speakers; pupils make their comments to the teacher rather than to the rest of the class or group; the teacher chairman, sometimes unconsciously, imposes restraint on what the pupils feel they can say. It cannot be felt that class discussion has been a great success if only five or six people take part in it; there is obviously value in listening, but one of the positive aspects of class discussion should be the number of participants. Similarly, comments aimed at the teacher chairman inhibit fluid discussion among the pupils and there is also a sense that he somehow knows the answer and this can limit the pupils as well.

At the start of this chapter a form of class discussion was mentioned different from the sort perhaps more frequently used; instead of the teacher trying to direct the discussion himself a pupil chairman was used. It was precisely because class discussions seemed to suffer from the restrictions just mentioned that this method was tried and it also made the comparison of small- and large-group work easier because it removed the influence of the teacher to some degree. Seating the class in a circle round the outside of the room facing inwards with the teacher on the outside of this circle, taking notes on what was said but not speaking, kept his presence sufficiently unobtrusive for the three disadvantages just mentioned to be considerably reduced. In two typical class discussions, one with a teacher chairman and one with a pupil chairman, nine people took part in the former and fourteen in the latter. The pupils seemed to feel less inhibited and did discuss with each other rather than addressing their comments to the teacher for approval. One of the many written comments made by pupils who discussed in this way helps to sum up the effect: 'If no teacher is chairing, the shyer people might get more confidence to join in the discussion, and people are often more polite and restrained if the teacher is chairman so they do not put their point of view across properly.'

This method has been described since it was largely in class discussions of this kind that the characteristics mentioned earlier were most apparent and also because it did seem to reduce some of the disadvantages and make class discussion as potentially useful as small-group discussion. However, despite the apparent advantages, there is one point that would seem to be a big disadvantage. If a pupil leads the discussion, instead of a teacher, what happens to the sense of direction and purpose? Guidance is surely what the teacher is there to give and if he does not give it, can the pupils provide their own?

Listening to the tapes of class discussion to see whether there was a lack of direction was interesting; occasionally there were examples of the sort of logical progression from point to point that a teacher might try to encourage were he leading, but there were many repetitions. To an outsider listening to such tapes, and even to the people involved in the discussion listening to the tape afterwards, this was noticeable and the reaction was to condemn it. However, this feeling that things had not gone well did not always match up with the group's understanding of the discussion as it happened; at the time it had seemed to work. The following example may help to explain this contradiction.

At the end of a discussion about some poems, the class was asked to consider the use of discussion. They considered this problem in a discussion that at the time seemed sensible and was very lively, but examination of a five minute section of the transcript showed the same point being made at least five times. (The comments have been edited to cut out interruptions and asides.) The pupil chairman started by asking: 'What is the use of discussion?'

ALAN To be able to understand what the play/what the poem's about easier/ 'cos you get more ideas.

Later on:

JANE To hear other people's opinions.

Later on:

JENNIFER But you've got to be able to hear both sides of an argument about things.

Later on:

HEATHER I think that when you're discussing poetry/well I think you get different views of poetry.

Later on:

TINA Everyone's got different viewpoints about things so you hear absolutely fresh views from your own.

It is not strictly true, of course, that these five contributions all made the same point. In each case a slightly different group of words was used, a group that fitted that particular person's perceptions, and as the words changed so did the idea. To call this repetition is perhaps wrong; restatement might be more accurate. This seems to be a good feature of discussion rather than one of the disadvantages to which a teacher has to resign himself. Restating an idea that has already been expressed by someone else is surely one of the most important ways in which we make ideas our own; as soon as the idea we have in our abstract perception is given the form of words it becomes easier to understand, it becomes visible. This might be one of the major reasons for encouraging discussion, whether in small or in large groups.

The example and comments do not suggest that there *is* a sense of direction; they merely point out a possible useful function of the dithering that might be considered *lack* of direction; they point to a way of interpreting some of the features that appear in pupil-chaired discussion. The actual business of moving from point to point, progressing from one idea to another, is something that a teacher can bring about himself by careful instructions or guidelines beforehand, by making the class aware of the possible ground to be covered.

A brief example might be useful. Stevie Smith's 'Not Waving but Drowning' was mentioned earlier. This poem was discussed in conjunction with two others: 'Survivors' by Alan Ross and 'The Rescue' from *Wodwo* by Ted Hughes. The class was given the poems to discuss in small groups first, was told in which order to read the poems and was given one or two questions about each. In the case of 'Not Waving but Drowning' the pupils were asked to work out who was speaking, in the hope that this would make them look at the basic literal meaning of the poem. Later on in the class discussion they were asked to consider rather more general questions in relation to the poems. They had to consider why Stevie Smith's poem had been given that title. The assumption was that after feeling some certainty about the basic meaning they would be able to consider metaphorical meanings. For this particular class these turned out to be the right guidelines and the discussion seemed to be useful and interesting as a result. One of the pupils writing about pupil-led discussion expressed it like this: 'One point about the discussions we have had is that if we are given a few guidelines and we know the subject we are to be discussing, well then we benefit a lot, but if no guidelines are given then the discussions drop in standard and people don't learn so much as they would if guidelines were given.'

Besides this, some sort of summing up by the teacher of the main points that have been made is useful as it rounds off the discussion in an organized way, showing the class how they have used the guidelines and helping them to feel that they have actually achieved something. Five minutes can be spent at the end going over the points that they seemed to consider important, perhaps picking out any points that appeared to have been discarded too easily and also commenting on the actual level of discussion – whether they had been listening and arguing well, for example.

Small groups have been used as preparation for the large group and there seem to be three reasons why this can work quite well.

First, the small groups give everyone the opportunity to work out their position, to sort out meanings, to define their opinions. They are well suited to this sort of process, as was suggested earlier on, and once discussion of this sort has taken place pupils will probably feel more confident about joining in the whole-class discussion. This is what seemed to help Neville in making his contribution to the class discussion about 'Not Waving but Drowning'.

NEVILLE We worked out that ummm/reckon it means that ummm/everyone thought he was all right/doing well/when he wasn't.

The fact that he referred his comments back to the common understanding they reached in their small group suggests that this was one of the sources of his confidence.

Second, the small groups provide a sympathetic audience whose reaction will help in considering how best to present the points that are to be made. They provide a useful rehearsal time for the much more public performance that may be made later on. This is another important way in which the small-group discussion can help to provide the confidence needed to join in the large group.

Third, the small groups can help to create the right sort of atmosphere for the large-group discussion, a feeling that there is something worth while to be talked about and that it is valuable to hear the opinions of others.

In conclusion, it can be said that large-group discussion work has a place alongside small-group work in the classroom. It would appear from this study that it is best suited to a slightly different purpose, one which has more to do with formal aspects of discussion and the conscious consideration of the process of exchanging ideas, and that problems relating to class size and teacher presence can be overcome.

V. Talk as part of the activity of learning

During the project's two-year life a large number of classroom recordings of children's talk was made: only a small proportion of these was transcribed, and a fraction of this has been used as illustrative material in the preceding chapters. The purpose of this chapter is to present in the form of an anthology some of the transcriptions made of work in progress both in English lessons and in those of subjects other than English, together with comments on the work and the transcripts. It is hoped that this material will serve as a stimulus to readers to undertake research of their own in one or two areas.

Examples are considered under the following headings:

1 *Use of talk in English lessons*
i Vocabulary work
ii Interviewing
iii Comprehensions:
    a Use of cloze comprehension to encourage talk within close limits
    b Use of cloze comprehension to encourage discussion and communication
    c Question-and-answer comprehension to stimulate group discussion
    d Discussion based on the 'comprehension' of a whole story
iv The beginnings of literary criticism
v Making up a story together.

2 *Use of talk in subjects other than English*
i Metalwork
ii Mathematics: long division
iii Mathematics: long division and the interpretation of graphs
iv Mathematics: learning to ask the right questions
v Science: a science teacher's 'circus' method.

1 Use of talk in English lessons

i VOCABULARY WORK

A teacher who had been reading John Steinbeck's *Of Mice and Men* with a fourth-year class decided to set a vocabulary exercise rather than a comprehension exercise to help pupils make a limited response to their reading. The teacher asked the children to get together in groups of from three to six. He then asked them to choose four characters from the novel, and to find the five best adjectives to describe each one. The teacher's aim was to make them think about each of the characters in a tightly organized way, in preparation for subsequent more extensive work on character study.

When the tape-recording of one group's discussion was examined, it showed how they had arrived at some of their answers:

a They needed to make clear to themselves what an adjective is:

JIM George/he's got brains.
PETER That doesn't describe him though/describing word is it?
FRED It's 'brainy'.

That little interchange shows them moving from a sentence ('he's got brains') to a single adjective ('brainy').

b They had been asked to describe the people's characteristics, so when one of the group suggested 'short', one of the others said 'No, describe their *minds* more.'

They perceived a difference between a word which is physically descriptive and one which is descriptive of character. They went on to look at 'character' words, as can be seen in **c**.

c In order to see whether a word was appropriate they needed to discuss the definition. Someone suggested that the stable-buck Crocks is lonely because he is black, but the group wanted a better word than 'lonely':

JIM What does 'conscious' mean?
PETER Self-conscious.
JIM Does that mean completely separate just 'cos he's black?
PETER He's got it on his mind all the time/he's aware of it/himself.

They arrived at a definition of 'self-conscious' which satisfied them so they could put the word down on their list.

d They looked for synonyms to help them clarify meanings to themselves: 'mean' they defined as 'tight'; 'childish' they saw as meaning 'dumb'. They tried to find one word which means 'his brain wasn't properly developed'; they tried 'wet', 'childish' and 'babyish' and tried unsuccessfully to find a word to fit together with 'mentally . . .', but failed to find the word 'defective'.

e They extended the activity at the last part of **d** in an attempt to find single words for phrases: 'he stays in the background . . .'; 'someone who's got a sensible outlook on life . . .'. They did not succeed in finding words that meant these things, but they went for the dictionary to try to do so.

Having been asked to talk about their answers rather than write them down in silence this group was able both to share each other's ideas and to challenge them. The final list of adjectives was achieved through a lively discussion of some of the memorable points of the novel.

Thus a task which involved working within a limited framework generated the kind of discussion which the group should be capable of conducting once they have had some experience of talking together.

ii INTERVIEWING

Rather than simply asking children to talk about something they might otherwise have done silently, it is valuable to give them tasks which necessarily involve both talking and listening. One such task is interviewing.

It seems preferable that such interviewing should take place outside the school. In one school a class was asked to make up questions to ask their own teacher and a visiting teacher to find out as much as they could about them. The artificiality of the situation led them to ask questions which did not demonstrate genuine interest in the subject of the interview. For example, they asked: 'What colour of socks do you wear?,' 'Have you got hairy legs?' and other questions designed to provoke a laugh from the rest of the class rather than to obtain genuine information.

A class in another school was asked to work on the topic 'What Life Was Like Twenty Years Ago'. This meant that the pupils had to work together initially to make up lists of suitable questions, go out and ask these questions and report back to the class afterwards. All these activities necessarily involved both talking and listening, and served to demonstrate to the children that talking is *necessary*. They were asked to make up questions which they could ask parents or grandparents or people in the shopping precinct, whichever they preferred to do. Those who had tape-recorders could make use of these at home.

One group went out with the school tape-recorder into the shopping precinct. They were third-year boys from a mixed-ability class. They stopped an old man and asked, 'Do you mind if we interview you?' to which he replied, 'A couple of minutes, perhaps.' The interview went on:

RALPH How long have you lived in Nailsea?

MAN Oh about nineteen years.

RALPH Has it changed much since you lived here?

MAN Oh it certainly has/it was pretty well all fields when I came here.

RALPH How much has transport changed since you were a child?

MAN Since I was a child?

RALPH Yeah.

MAN Well it was all horses and carts in those days/you 'aven't got no recorder on now/yes you 'ave/'aven't you?

RALPH Yes.

MAN Oh I thought you 'ad.

RALPH What sort of jobs were available when you left school?

MAN God knows, I don't/I never inquired/almost as soon as I left school I was/er/had to be in the army.

RALPH How has social life changed in the last twenty years?

MAN Oh wonderful really for the masses of people since the First World War.

RALPH What were the wages like twenty years ago for jobs?

MAN Oh really starvation/for the jobs/everything was the same/plenty of everything here but the people/you know/the ordinary working people had a job to find a job to get a livin'/we worked the clock right round to get nothing almost.

(*Break in tape*)

I was a choir boy and I went twice a day Sunday morning and the evening and Sunday afternoons to Sunday school/pretty well everyone done the same.

RALPH Did you go on any school outing or camps or things like that?

MAN Yes we were taken away once a year down to the seaside down as far as Weston and all like that/then the Sunday School/the choir boys we were taken away on to the seaside down as far as Weymouth/which you all looked forward to all over the year/right through the year/looked forward to these little outings/it was only after the First World War that things began to alter for the mass of people/before then the mass of people their education was nil/absolutely nil/now/lookin' back from my day now/it has altered wonderful so that everyone now has got a chance of a good time.

The interview continued at length. The interviewer not only had to talk, but he also had to *listen* which, as was suggested above, is as important a function of communication through talking as talking is itself.

Another pair of boys talked to an old man who remembered the time when horse-carts used to take Bristolians on day-excursions to Weston-super-Mare, stopping in Nailsea for a half-way pint: he and his friends used to rush out and sell flowers to the trippers. Thus the children discovered that talk had the interesting function of eliciting real information.

iii COMPREHENSIONS

'Comprehension' in English generally refers to exercises and tests which are set to see whether children have understood a text or can understand a given extract. In the context of the work of this project, comprehension is also used to refer to the understanding and appreciation of whole poems and stories after a lengthy period of talking and writing about them. We suggest in this section that the process of *talking* through a comprehension *exercise* to a very limited brief has two functions: getting children used to the idea of talking things out; and demonstrating to them that group work can lead to enhanced understanding.

a *Use of cloze comprehension to encourage talk within close limits*
The first example given is of a 'cloze' comprehension set with a very limited and narrow purpose in mind. The activity involves the discussion of which word would be most suitable to fill a gap in a piece of writing based on an understanding of the context gained from careful reading of the existing text. In terms of children talking together, then, this is a valuable way of getting them to discuss the different possibilities.

The cloze exercise quoted below was set to a class which had found it very difficult to use talk constructively. They had come into the third-year English classes at the beginning of the year in an unsettled frame of mind and they demonstrated that they did not think that there was any purpose to talking in class other than that of actively and noisily wasting time. The teacher managed to get them to work silently for a time and read John Steinbeck's *The Pearl* to them partly in an attempt to encourage them to *listen.*

After the book had been read the teacher decided to give them a cloze exercise based on the book, with the very limited purpose of encouraging them to begin to talk effectively together. The example given shows two boys working at a very superficial level of understanding: it was not expected that at this stage they would be capable of achieving a greater depth of understanding, simply that they would be encouraged to begin to realize that talking together for reasons other than disruption is possible in the classroom.

The extract used is from near the end of *The Pearl*. The story is about a native pearl-fisher who has found the most magnificent pearl in all the world; the pearl brings him no happiness since it attracts the greed of all around; he has been forced to kill for it, and to run away from his village with his wife and child. But he is pursued and, at the point of the extract, he is turning on his pursuers to try to kill them before they kill him. The words missed out are: (1) rock, (2) sought, (3) even, (4) slip.

The teacher told the class that they did not have to find the exact words: simply words which to them seemed to fit the context:

> TEACHER You and your partner are going to find out what words will fit/you don't have to find the exact words/you may well come up with the exact words . . . in other cases you may be choosing a word which according to your memory, your understanding/will fit in that place.

The extract used was as follows:

Kino edged like a slow lizard down the smooth rock shoulder. He had turned his neck-string so that the great knife hung down from his back and could not clash against the stones. His spread fingers gripped the __(1)__ and his bare toes __(2)__ support through contact, and __(3)__ his chest lay against the rock so that he would not __(4)__ .

The class was divided into pairs which in most cases were simply the way the children were already sitting together. Martin and Steven were taped because they had already had experience of the tape-recorder in mathematics lessons the previous year, but none in English.

1 MARTIN That one must be 'rocks' right?/'Gripped' the rocks whatever it is/right?/'and his bare toes . . .'/what?
2 STEVEN 'And his bare toes . . .'
3 MARTIN 'Something support through contact.'
4 STEVEN That/that's/it's not . . .
5 MARTIN Could be/it's all right/'sought' or 'thought through contact' and 'support through contact'/it's something like that isn't it?/when you think about it.
6 STEVEN Yeah/we'll leave that/'and his . . .'/oh.
(Interruption from another group)
21 MARTIN Right/right/'And something his chest lay against the rock'/put 'rock'/again/right.
22 STEVEN Yeah/'so that he would not fall . . .'/no?
23 MARTIN 'So that he would not be seen'.
24 STEVEN Can it be two words?
(They seek guidance from the teacher)

The word 'rocks' (1) was found with ease; Martin found a rhyming as well as a contextual justification for 'sought' (2); the blank space at (3) was left until other words had been filled in and they could come back and find the word 'even'. At (4) the two boys veered between 'fall' and 'be seen'; they could only allow themselves to use 'be seen' if the teacher said they could use two words.

Thus they were beginning to work together, offering but not yet justifying alternative ideas, and both (at the interruption) rejecting attempts by another group to stop them from working. All these elements must be present if effective working together in groups is to take place.

From this point onwards that particular class became more and more capable of working together. The extract quoted was made at the beginning of the period during which the pupils actively co-operated with each other and with the teacher to produce some very fine work. The work did not include other cloze comprehension. The very limited requirement imposed on the cloze comprehension at this point had been fulfilled: it had encouraged the children to begin talking effectively together.

b *Use of cloze comprehension to encourage discussion and communication*
The next extract shows cloze being used in a different school more specifically for the purpose of comprehension, and with much greater effectiveness towards that end. Two girls were looking at two passages from a Gapadol Reading Comprehension exercise. The sentence they are considering is from 'A Description of Leamas': His —— were brown and small. The girls did not immediately arrive at the correct answer, but one of the purposes of cloze is to encourage the discussion and justification of various alternatives: they found some and rejected one at [4] by referring to a point earlier in the passage.

1 SAMANTHA 'His eyes, his neck.'
2 RACHEL No his legs. (*laughter*)
3 SAMANTHA 'His something were brown and small'/(*giggles*)/'his hair was brown and small.'
4 RACHEL No/'cos he's got iron-grey hair.
5 SAMANTHA His body/his body.
6 RACHEL 'Brown and small.'
7 SAMANTHA No/yes.
8 LESLEY (*She is writing the words down*) 'His body was brown and small?'
9 RACHEL Right/come on then.

They did not realize that they had missed a context clue by changing 'were' to 'was', so they went on to the consideration of other words, apparently satisfied. Five minutes later (at utterances [85] to [88] on the transcript) when they were stuck on a word in the middle of the next passage (which was about turtles), Lesley, who appeared to have carried the former problem in her head (perhaps because she was 'secretary') suddenly arrived at the correct word. All her companions immediately switched back to the previous passage, and, judging by their laughter at their former insertion of the word 'body', accepted Lesley's alternative.

> 85 LESLEY (*Suddenly and with emphasis*) 'Eyes were brown and small'/oh/ sorry!
> 86 RACHEL Can't be eyes/(*she is still working on the turtles passage*)/'Eyes were brown and small.' (*realization*)
> 87 SAMANTHA Body!!
> 88 RACHEL Body!! (*general laughter*)

The girls had set up a pattern of communication within the group by means of which understanding was transmitted without the need for explanation: one clue from Lesley enabled them to switch back immediately to an earlier phase of their work.

c *Question-and-answer comprehension to stimulate group discussion*
Another form of comprehension exercise which can be done in pairs or groups is the more common question-and-answer type. The value of doing such exercises as part of group activities would seem to be limited to preparing the group for further and more extensive ways of studying texts, rather than as an end in itself. The example, as with the cloze example **a** above, shows discussion at an embryonic stage. It shows those basic elements of group work which are likely to develop into fruitful co-operation as the group learns to work together.

The group had read a comprehension passage about the way in which Galileo was led to think more deeply about pendulums by a chance experience in the cathedral at Pisa:

> Suddenly something caught his eye. Some workmen who were making repairs to the building had set the great central lamp swinging. Fascinated, Galileo rose and watched it. Strange! It started swinging in a wide arc, but as the arc of its swing became smaller its swinging became slower.

The boys had to answer the question, 'What chance enabled Galileo to start thinking about pendulums while in the cathedral at Pisa?' Sean's answer was as follows

> SEAN It was a fluke!
> SIMON What's that mean?

SEAN Like when you score a goal/right?/in football/and you don't know you're going to score it/right?/say it comes off your foot accidentally/right?

SIMON It was an accident then?/'cos he walked into the church because he wanted to see the pretty altars and hanging pictures and that/and he saw . . .

SAUL And dirty pictures!

SEAN It was a complete and utter fluke.

SAUL Just by chance he happened to walk in and started up and said, 'Ah, there's something swinging – it's a pendulum!'

Sean was demonstrating an occurrence which is observed quite frequently in tapes of group talk: that one member of the group tries to explain to another something the other does not understand. It is far less important that the explanation seems in some way to degrade the experience by being couched in colloquial terminology, than that one boy is *willing* to offer an explanation to another who does not understand: Sean was adopting a teaching role in the group.

Another thing which can be observed going on in this exchange (and observed much more readily when the complete transcript is read in conjunction with the complete tape) is that the explanation was not accepted fully by another member of the group: Simon would seem to have accepted the explanation, whereas Saul chose to make fun of it, either because he did not like the word 'fluke' or because he did not believe that Galileo's discovery could have been as easy as is suggested in the passage. In this case Saul was seen to be at a very early stage in the process of trying to interpret the whole text: whether or not he could go on from there would depend both on the ability of the group to develop a good working relationship and on the skill of the teacher in presenting them with more challenging activities.

d *Discussion based on the 'comprehension' of a whole story*

It has been observed several times above that both cloze and question-and-answer comprehension exercises undertaken in the ways illustrated have limited value. If the idea of 'comprehension' is to be extended to mean accomplishing an understanding of a whole text, then it must not be limited to such exercises.

Thus, although one might start in such a way, it would be inappropriate to remain at that point. Some textbooks offer questions for discussion which could lead groups to examine wider issues than those simply presented in a short literary extract. Such discussions are likely to depend on the textbook compiler's skill in choosing just the right extract. We have certainly found it more effective to base 'comprehension' work on complete stories rather than on textbook extracts. The quality of discussion is likely to be enhanced because the participants have much more to go on, to which they can refer explicitly by consulting the text, or implicitly by bringing to the discussion their own experience of the whole story which they can relate to their wider experience of life.

A group of boys had just read Isaac Asimov's story 'The Fun They Had', in which children of the twenty-second century suppose that school was much more fun in the days when there were human teachers rather than the robot teachers which they have in their own homes. The boys (third-year mixed ability) were asked to discuss the following question in small groups:

QUESTION Would you prefer a robot teacher to the present system?

ANDREW The school teacher in the story wasn't so good as nowadays because you can't get a good relationship with your teacher/sort of thing . . .

BRENDAN You can't have a laugh.

CHARLES I think it would be better to have a modern-day teacher/like they were a sort of robot teacher/because it would be better/because you can't build up much of a relationship with the teachers of nowadays (*meaning, it seems, 'nowadays' in the twenty-second century*).

BRENDAN Nowadays I think it is best to have a group of people because you can't really work on your own/you must get so sick of it that you won't want to work/and you'll keep on leaving it/so you'll say/I'll catch on the next day.

CHARLES Sometimes the teacher takes a dislike to you straight away which is not very good/the robot teacher can't take a dislike to you because he has not got a brain.

The boys were actively using ideas from the science-fiction story to think more carefully about their own situation: if you were to have to work on your own you would have less motive for working than when in competition with a group; you cannot establish a relationship with a robot; on the other hand, a robot cannot take a dislike to you but a teacher can, and so on. Thus their understanding of the passage was enhanced by their feelings about their own experience.

iv THE BEGINNINGS OF LITERARY CRITICISM

In the following example, a class had listened to the tape-recording of a BBC presentation of *Dracula*. Ten minutes before the end of the lesson they were asked to write down five points for and five points against the story. The boys were in their fourth year in the secondary school, soon to be put into a fifth-year class which would work towards CSE English literature. It was hoped that this kind of discussion would later enable them to indulge in a deeper and more extensive examination of literary texts; here they were not tied down too tightly to a specific question, rather they were limited by the time factor.

MALCOLM Think of a third point *for* the story.
PETER Right/um.
MALCOLM Um.
PETER Now let's see/what did . . .
MALCOLM Yeah/when he put all that garlic in and/started to wonder what it was for/and the wolves and the silver dust.
PETER The silver dust.
MALCOLM I liked that.
PETER The silver dust came in every . . .
MALCOLM What is it anyway?
PETER Well it/you know/silver dust or what you saw all the way through it/ every time something dramatic was going to happen it always is/dramatic/ like, dramatic when Lucy had the dream.
MALCOLM Silver dust.
PETER And silver dust when he was in the castle/and silver dust when Lucy was just about to . . .
MALCOLM I reckon that was Dracula.

Implicitly, it would seem, by their references to the recurrence of silver dust in the story, the pupils had sensed that one point in favour of the story was that it is well-structured: Peter noticed that silver dust came into the story 'every time something dramatic was going to happen', and Malcolm related this to Dracula's ability to change his shape and appear when and where he wanted to. Thus they found themselves not only talking about the story, but going beyond it: not to their own experiences, but to an external view of the structure of the story.

V MAKING UP A STORY TOGETHER

Groups of children in a third-year mixed-ability class were asked to make up a long story together. It is an activity which calls on a multiplicity of skills, involving much more than simply talking together. It was necessary to provide positive limits within which the group had to work. In the example given below this was done in the following way: the teacher started by giving them an example of how a story can be structured, using the five acts of a Shakespeare play as a basis. In Act 1 the scene is set, characters introduced, past events referred to and the action set going; in Act 2 the action develops with the addition of complications; Act 3 includes the 'point of no return' in the play (where Julius Caesar is murdered, or where Othello becomes insanely jealous, for example); Act 4 produces the inevitable consequences of Act 3; and this in its turn leads to the climax of the story in Act 5. The teacher offered his own simple example of a story in five acts: Act 1 – a boy sets out from home on a bicycle which he knows has defective brakes; Act 2 – he cycles up a hill; Act 3 – he comes to the top of the steep descent, looks at his defective brakes, but decides he will risk going down; Act 4 – he accelerates down the hill until he reaches a speed of thirty or forty miles per hour; Act 5 – he suddenly encounters a car overtaking a lorry on a bend and cannot avoid crashing headlong into the lorry. The teacher added other limitations suggested by the Greek 'unities': time, place and action should be severely limited. Then the children were asked to write their story, basing it round five photographs (one for each act or chapter) with themselves as participants in the story. Finally, they were to record their finished stories with added sound effects, to produce a tape–slide sequence.

The tendency was for the third-year children given this work to fantasize madly at first about their imagined experiences, turning each idea for a still photograph into an extract from a cine-film. It was only when they had learnt to control their fantasies that they were able to work effectively together.

Eventually the groups wrote their stories which they recorded in a studio with a separate tape-recorder 'listening' to each group working. One of the boys who wrote the stories said in his report of the work:

> We started at the beginning of the term by writing up three ideas. Then we were organized into groups and we then chose just one idea from each person. There was a vote to see which one we would use. Once we had decided we started to write it out in script form. We were told we had to write it out in story form so as to have practice in punctuation. When we had done this I was told that mine lacked narrative, so I tried again adding description of objects, places and people. Then we wrote a list of sound effects and picture scenes. We then had the problem of 'he is saying less than I am' and so we wanted each other's parts. So we all changed and tried again . . .

It can be seen from this account that the writing itself involved a considerable amount of discussion in the groups, which encouraged self-criticism of their own work and methods. Malcolm had this to say of the recording:

> We had to keep changing the script because we kept saying each other's lines and we would have spent half the time arguing if we had not realized what we were doing.

A tape had been played all throughout working to see how we worked and what problems we had.

The activity of tape-recording involved, according to Malcolm, the need to discover a way of working which avoided argument. This alone is good, showing that the activity strongly motivated the boys to work well. In addition we see Malcolm adopting a teaching role at [4] and [7] below, and we see the boys discussing the way they sound on the tape-recorder (at [1], [3] and [9]), obviously having lost all tape-recorder shyness.

1 PETER How come I sound very funny on this tape when you lot are all right?

2 MALCOLM That's because/do you know what?

3 ROBERT You all seem to sound the same to me.

4 MALCOLM That's because/you know what?/you all sound different simply because you're hearing it differently/when we hear you you sound different/ you sound like you sound/right?/but when you hear it you hear it from the inside/your ears and your mouth.

5 PETER Hold on/I've got to write picture one in.

6 NEVILLE Picture one is of you two boys.

7 MALCOLM Your mouth and your ears are all connected up/so you hear it from the inside/do/do you get it, Peter?

8 PETER Yes.

9 MALCOLM That's everybody thinks the same/everybody thinks/'why do I sound funny'/but they sound all right.

10 NEVILLE ... sound deeper/(*deep voice imitating games master*)/up down up down.

Peter was only partly listening to what Malcolm had to say because he was really more interested in getting on with the task [5]. As soon as that brief episode was over that was what they did, and the boys reverted to a concise work dialogue directed to fitting the script together with the sound effects on the recording.

11 MALCOLM Right then/now you Rob/you speak now then we'll continue on.

12 NEVILLE Hold on.

13 MALCOLM Just start here without the tape running/go on.

14 ROBERT 'Hello you two.'

15 MALCOLM Yeah.

16 ROBERT (*Acting*) 'Hello you two, come on in.'

17 PETER (*Softly*) Picture one.

18 MALCOLM Right, then we can have the door shutting again/all right?/ (*makes sound effect with voice*)/right that's shutting/so, ready?/ready Rob?

19 NEVILLE Ah no! no no no no ...

20 MALCOLM Yeah, 'cos we're going to have the door shutting aren't we?
21 PETER Oi! be silent!/now.
22 ROBERT 'Hello you two, come on in.'

This joint exercise brought in many aspects of English. They were here reading from their carefully written story, and thinking while they worked of the audience to whom they would play the story and show the pictures. They had to learn to work together, evolving a concise and effective style of work talk, and learning to criticize their efforts in conjunction with one another and with the teacher. They were capable of adopting a teaching role when it was called for, as a natural part of their working dialogue.

2   Use of talk in subjects other than English

i   METALWORK

The constant noise in a metalwork shop would seem to make it an unlikely place to study talk. What such a study does is to bring into sharp focus the fact that talk has its proper place among a multitude of learning experiences, and that while it is necessary to talk at some times, at others it is impracticable and even dangerous.

Noise, heat, smell, the touch and feel of materials and the vibration of machinery all provide a physical experience in which talking plays a minor but very significant part. When someone is engaged on an operation, that task demands total concentration, making any diversion in the form of talking or any other distraction inappropriate and even dangerous.

This point was demonstrated to the observer in a very positive way. Rather than simply watch what was going on, he asked to be given a job to do, and was given a standard metalwork exercise: making a garden-line winder. At one point he was heating a metal rod in the forge prior to beating a point onto it, but feeling guilty that he was not doing his 'proper' job of observing, he began to make notes, only to have his attention suddenly called back to the forge when one of the children told him that his metal was on fire: indeed it was, with a superb display of sparks shooting off it. Perhaps, as a pupil, instead of making notes he might have been gossiping to one of his mates, and the result would have been the same: lack of attention in the metalwork shop can be dangerous and can cause work to be ruined.

Craft activities demand total concentration, so talking can only safely be indulged in before or after an operation, but not usually during it, unless it is to call someone's attention to a danger which is not apparent to him.

The teacher must talk in order to explain the safety rules carefully, and to reinforce them continually. He must also explain the specialized vocabulary of the craft, without which it would be quite easy to use the wrong tools, material or process.

There is still a valuable place for pupil talk. Because of the constant noise in the metalwork shop, children find that they can talk freely to one another and to the teacher without fear of being overheard. If a child has to admit a mistake or ignorance he is likely to feel embarrassed if the whole class is listening, so he may prefer to keep quiet; he probably does so very often in other subjects where classrooms are quieter. If he can talk to his friend (as in the example below), or to the teacher, without the possibility of being more generally heard then he is more likely to want to do so and to be open and frank while doing so. This is an indication that classroom noise in other lessons (usually the noise of other children talking) can actually free reticent children's inhibitions against talking and asking and answering questions.

The example which follows shows a piece of collaborative learning taking place between two pupils, in which the more experienced and capable of the two (Barry) helped his friend (Gerard) in a situation which they both readily accepted.

Gerard was preparing to drill a piece of metal on a huge fixed drilling machine, on which the drill was brought down onto the work on the workbench by pulling a lever. (The transcript is given in the form of single parallel comment on individual utterances – see Appendix A.)

1 GERARD Barry/which switches this contraption on?	Seeks information from his friend rather than the teacher.
2 BARRY The green button/green for go.	Both gives and reinforces information.
3 GERARD Green/red off?	Confirms that he has understood and expresses uncertainty.
4 BARRY Green for go sonny/you've got to get it all lined up, look/show what you should do.	Asserts his 'teaching' role. Reacts to Gerard's uncertainty. Offers help.
5 GERARD I know/I know.	Seems not to like being told; yet does not reject further offers of help.

(Machine noise makes some remarks inaudible)

6 BARRY Undo the nuts/*(inaudible)*/ done that yet?/pull it down/keep going/pull it down/the whole thing down/that's it/*(words inaudible)*/	Tells him how to bring the drill down onto the piece of metal.

keep going a bit more/a bit more than that/ah/that should do/that should do it actually/what are you doing with the/(*impatiently*)	Continues his instructions while Gerard does what he is told to do. Reacts to Gerard going wrong.
7 GERARD (*Inaudible*)	
8 BARRY Pull it down/that'll do now/	Gerard has located the position of the drill.
leave it like that/now you've got to line it up onto the block/that's easy enough.	Shows Gerard how to line up the drill with the piece of metal.
9 GERARD All right/all right!	Expresses impatience at Barry's continuing intervention.
10 BARRY Line it up with the block/ that's it/now, switch on/pull down/ and hold on this/otherwise it will go.	Gives safety instruction.
11 GERARD Right.	
12 BARRY It's not easy to know that/ (*conversationally with a slight laugh*)/I found that out/you have to hold on to it tight then.	Reminds himself of his own experience and tries to reassure Gerard. Reverts to 'teaching' tone.
(*Ten seconds of noise*)	Gerard hesitates.
13 GERARD (*Self-deprecating*) Oh I'll try it (*starts drill*).	Maintains his role as pupil.
14 BARRY Don't let go of that or it'll start moving.	Repeats safety instruction.
15 GERARD Mind you I wouldn't like to let go of it.	Shows he has understood Barry's instruction.
16 BARRY (*Chuckles*) No.	Reassures Gerard again.

Gerard's acceptance of his role as pupil in [9], [11] and [13] and the evident rapport between Barry and him in [14], [15] and [16] bear witness to the effectiveness of this teaching/learning situation. Barry had also consolidated his own knowledge by having had to explain it to Gerard: in both [10] and [12] he referred to his past experience, both to remind himself of what happened when he did this operation and to tell Gerard what to avoid. Neither might have accepted the teacher–pupil relationship if other members of the class had been listening to their every word. Later on, when the teacher was explaining how to scribe a curve on metal, and Barry said 'Yes' readily to the teacher's question 'Can you do that?', Gerard called Barry 'brains', yet he was happy to work with and to learn from Barry in the workshop, most probably because they were free to talk 'secretly' when the need arose.

When discussing the observations made in the metalwork lessons, the teacher said that the things he most wanted to know were:

i   What can I gain from understanding better what goes on in the lessons?

ii What contribution can that understanding make to my teaching?

iii How can I enable pupils to learn better through talk as part of the whole process?

To some extent he had already intuitively answered these questions. He insists positively on the need for care in a dangerous situation by making sure that children know and understand technical vocabulary; he allows pupils to work together and talk about their work where it is appropriate; he goes round the class talking to the children and listening to them talking about their work; he carefully explains processes to them and expects them to be able to tell him what they are doing. His method, he says, is not to tell the children everything, but to challenge them to find out for themselves: finding out involves both doing the work and talking about it.

There is one talk activity which might be made more use of both in metalwork and in other practical subjects. That is a time at the end of the lesson or of a series of lessons in which children are encouraged to talk about what they have learnt more widely than just in respect of its immediate practical application, attempting to find wider applications and implications so that they will not be at a loss when a problem of a slightly different nature arises later.

ii MATHEMATICS: LONG DIVISION
In the following example, three second-year pupils were working on a long-division exercise: Question (b) $3189 \div 0.24$ ($= 13\ 287.5$). Harry was helped considerably by being able to test his thoughts out verbally before committing them to paper (which he did at utterance [27]).

1 TOM Question (b) we have to do?
2 HARRY Yeah (b). (*pause*)
3 TOM You have to add two noughts onto it.
4 DICK You big flirt!
5 HARRY (*Reprovingly*) We're being recorded!
(*Pause*)
6 HARRY (*At work*) Eh?
7 TOM Pardon?

8 HARRY How do you make it that?
9 TOM 'Cos you move the decimal point along/don't you?
10 HARRY But there's no decimal point in it.
11 TOM There is.
12 HARRY There isn't/not in (b).
13 DICK (b)/there is.
14 HARRY Oh!
15 TOM Just add two noughts on to it (*pause*).
16 HARRY You don't 'ave to.
17 DICK That won't make any difference.
18 HARRY (*Agrees*) Won't make any difference/(*pause*)/no/it's 132 885/that's what mine made/where'd you get your sum from?
19 DICK Stanley!
20 STANLEY (*From another group*) Shut up!
21 TOM Now what?
22 DICK Hold it/don't bother/don't bother.
23 TOM Bring down the nought.
24 DICK Goes 7 times that/'cos 7 times 24 is 168.
25 TOM Then this time it should go in.
26 DICK That's a 7/it is, honest/(*correcting*)/7/then it goes a 5/it goes 7, 5/ you've missed out the 7. (*pause*)
27 HARRY Stanley's got/that means it's point 5 isn't it?/it's point 5?/it's point 5/it's that now/point 5.
28 DICK (c).
29 TOM Hold it/we have to do (c) in a minute/so it's 13 287·5.
30 DICK (b) 13 287·5.
31 TOM Now (c) we have to do.

This type of working is fairly common in mathematics lessons; although the boys all had the answer, 13 287·5, each one had in his own way co-operated in achieving that answer by being allowed to talk through the working.

There are, however, two dangers if this kind of exchange becomes routine without any built-in constraints:

a a dominant member of the group can force the others to accept his assumptions, even if they are incorrect;

b members of the group can soon start to do questions *in turn*, seldom bothering to check the correctness of the others' assumptions and working.

iii MATHEMATICS: LONG DIVISION AND THE INTERPRETATION OF GRAPHS

In the following example, two boys in a second-year setted mathematics class were tackling the problem of finding the average number of children per family in their class of thirty-four. They were given a bar graph showing the numbers of families with 1, 2, 3, 4 or 5 children (see Figure 2). To find the average number of children per family, they should have added up the total number of children represented in the five columns: 7 + 18 + 33 + 20 + 10 = 88, and divided this number by 34. This would have given them an answer of approximately 2·59.

In fact, the boys divided 15 (1 + 2 + 3 + 4 + 5) by 34. They did their long-division sum correctly, only to find finally that the answer was 0·4411, 'a funny odd number', in Martin's words. They failed to question the accuracy of their original assumption.

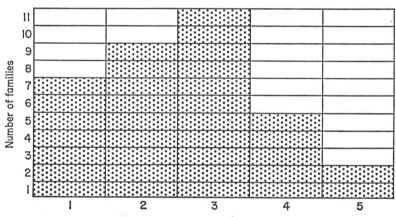

Fig. 2 Bar graph showing the numbers of families in a class and the number of children in each family

The transcript is set out with utterances on the left and the progress of the mathematical calculation on the right.

1 MARTIN The number of families is 34.   34

2 GEORGE Oh/I see what you mean/yes.

3 MARTIN And 34 into 15 doesn't go/so you put a nought on   34) 15
the end and put a decimal point in/34 into 150/about . . .   34) 150

$$\overset{\cdot 4}{34\,)\,\overline{150}}$$

4 GEORGE 4 times.   34) 150

5 MARTIN 4 times.

6 GEORGE I'm good at guessing.

7 MARTIN Try to work it out/now/four 4s are 16/1 to carry. $4 \times 34 = {}_16$

8 GEORGE Four 4s.

9 MARTIN Four 3s are 12/1/3/then you double that/then you go 4/10.

$$4 \times 34 = 136$$

$$34 \overline{\smash{\big)}\, 150} \atop \begin{array}{r} \cdot 4 \\ \hline 136 \\ \hline 14 \end{array}$$

10 GEORGE Really (*maybe he wonders what Martin meant by 'double that'*).

11 MARTIN Shut up!/1.

12 GEORGE Shh!

13 MARTIN 14/that's it/so put another nought there.

$$34 \overline{\smash{\big)}\, 150} \atop \begin{array}{r} \cdot 4 \\ \hline 136 \\ \hline 140 \end{array}$$

14 GEORGE Mind that/it's not another nought.

15 MARTIN And we put a 4 there.

$$34 \overline{\smash{\big)}\, 150} \atop {\cdot 44}$$

16 GEORGE It's a 444444 recurring.

17 MARTIN 1.

$$34 \overline{\smash{\big)}\, 150} \atop \begin{array}{r} \cdot 441 \\ \hline 136 \\ \hline 140 \\ 136 \\ \hline 40 \\ 34 \\ \hline \end{array}$$

18 GEORGE No that isn't a recurring/oh good/that's it/that's one/that's it/no it ain't.

Although Martin was doing most of the work, George was doing some as well: for example at [4], [8], [10] and especially [18]. Martin went on to complete the calculation to four places of decimals, getting 0·4411. But Martin was not satisfied since he called this 'a funny odd number'. He did not succeed, however, in finding out why it was funny. This, as the tape-transcript of later utterances revealed, was because he did not see the need to question it further.

iv MATHEMATICS: LEARNING TO ASK THE RIGHT QUESTIONS

If it is valuable for children to be encouraged to ask questions at appropriate points in their calculations, it is reasonable to ask how they can be enabled to do this. Martin, in example **iii**, did not know that he had to ask any more questions. One suggestion, made by Frankie Todd, is that the group play a 'game' in which one of them pretends to have been absent, and the others have to explain to him what they have done and what they have to do.

In the following example, an English teacher visiting a mathematics lesson explained this idea to a group of children in the same class as George and Martin doing an exercise on graphical interpretation. The transcript is set out with utterances on the left and position on the graph related to these utterances on the right.

1 TEACHER It's not just a game/it's/what we are wondering is whether doing it this way you yourself will get a clearer picture of what you're doing/making you talk about it and think about it/some of the mistakes that you might possibly make could be prevented by explaining to yourselves what you are doing.

2 NEVILLE Yeah!

3 ADRIAN Ah!

4 TEACHER Would you like to do that now? (*He points to School Mathematics Project Book D, exercise D on graphical interpretation, question 1 on figure 8, p. 148 – see below.*)

The figure shows the sad story of a boy trying to catch a bus. Describe what you think happened

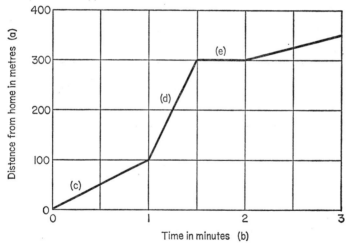

If he had gone at the same speed all the time, what would that speed have been? (Use the graph to help you.) Draw the line that represents this steady speed.

5 ADRIAN Okay/what do we do then?/have a look in here/hello/where are we?/no.

(*Adrian turns to the exercise in the book before he begins to explain to Neville who has to pretend to have been absent.*)

6 ADRIAN Well look/this boy walks off/that is up there the distance he goes/see? (a)

7 NEVILLE Yeah.

8 ADRIAN And that's the time/and the shallower the angle the slower (b)
he walks.

9 NEVILLE What?/the higher the quicker?

10 ADRIAN Yeah/so that if he walks along there/look/if he goes up there
he's travelled 100 metres in one minute/ (c)
and he goes the next 200 in half a minute/ (d)
and he must be a very fast runner because he does the next 200 in
half a minute.

11 NEVILLE Yeah/go on.

12 ADRIAN But when he comes along here he travels 100 metres in one
minute/ (c)
and he goes the next 200 in half a minute/ (d)
so he's a dead fast runner.

13 NEVILLE Yeah.

14 ADRIAN If it's er/on this sort of graph/it's a straight line/it shows the
distance from home is/it means that he stays still. (e)

15 NEVILLE What/so he stays still for half a minute then . . .

Unfortunately, just as Neville was beginning to respond as he should
have done had he played his part of the 'game' properly, Adrian plunged
into his explanation of the next question they had done, which was question
3 in the same exercise on graphical interpretation from *SMP Book D*.
Perhaps with more careful preparation he could have got Neville to tell the
'sad story' as the question demanded.

Question 3 was as follows:

Make up a story, giving as much detail as you can, to explain the graph
below.

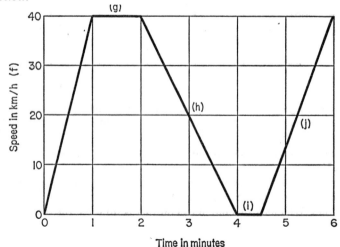

Time in minutes

Adrian continued without interruption from Neville:

16 ADRIAN Yeah/but on this one he/that shows he's/ this one's showing
his speed/ (f)
and this one shows that/the flat bit there shows that his speed stays
the same/ (g)
and this bit here/instead of showing his returning home shows his
speed dropping/ (h)
then he stops altogether/ (i)
then he goes off again/ (j)
get it?
17 NEVILLE Yeah.
18 ADRIAN Right/thank you.
19 NEVILLE That was a nice little game/wasn't it?

The exercise may have been helpful to Adrian, although he did not push himself far enough to enable him to recognize any mistakes he might have made originally. Neville needed to develop a more articulate response than 'yeah'.

This is merely a suggested and largely untried method, involving what Barnes and Todd refer to as reflexivity: the ability to reflect on what you are doing, so that, by questioning, mistakes arising from false assumptions may be avoided. Further research could well be done on this method, since the two examples quoted above show it in its very embryonic form.

V SCIENCE: A SCIENCE TEACHER'S 'CIRCUS' METHOD

A chemistry teacher provided examples of his own talk methods in chemistry lessons. The teacher concerned had been using these methods for many years throughout the school, and was not associated with the work of this project. No transcripts were available. He described the procedure as follows:

Surely all science teachers now do a lot of 'circus' work? You have small groups of children doing various experiments round the laboratory all dealing with different aspects of the same theme (for example, energy, light, air, water). As the groups finish you get them, in turn, to present their findings and conclusions orally to the rest of the class, and gradually lead them to see the connecting ideas underlying the experiments. This oral part where I draw everything together is the culmination of a sequence of lessons where other methods are used as well, and I see it as an indispensable part of the learning process.

A more detailed breakdown of such a sequence follows: this one dealt with energy, and was with a fifth-year option group, but the method used would basically be the same with all ages and abilities.

Stage 1: opening lesson
This was mainly teacher talk. The teacher outlined the topics to be explored with copious references to past knowledge. He asked the questions:

a Why do chemical reactions take place at all?
   Why do certain factors seem essential before reactions will occur?
   Why do reactions *not* occur at times?
b Why is heat generated by some reactions?
   Why do some reactions depend on applied heat?

The clue given was *energy*. The next task was to decide what the energy was doing.

Stage 2: group work
The class was divided into five groups. Each group was given details of an experiment they had to do. The teacher briefly summarized his instructions and the goals of the practical work. He estimated the work would occupy the subsequent $2\frac{1}{2}$ lessons ($2 \times 40 + 20 = 100$ min). He said: 'This work will involve revision, careful measurement, reading and discussion.'

Stage 3: whole-class discussion
At the end of the next double period, two groups had finished and had some puzzling results. The teacher stopped the remaining groups and made the two groups who had finished explain their results and their problems to the class. Suggestions and theories then came from the class. (The teacher admitted that there was a problem in keeping the future A-level pupils interested until the slower ones had understood the problems.) In this instance the class arrived *with no help from the teacher* at the correct explanations.

This was exceptionally successful. Normally the teacher listens to the class discussion very carefully and expects to have to feed in clues from time to time and occasionally rescue the class from a 'blind alley' resulting from the limitations of their knowledge of chemistry at this stage. This class discussion method takes more time but results in better understanding, he feels. Nevertheless, pressure of the syllabus is such that the teacher has an urgent responsibility to ensure the discussion is as productive as possible. Hence he must act as 'watchdog' in the way described, though resisting the temptation to intervene unnecessarily.

Stage 4: stage 2 continued

Meanwhile, the other groups were still wrestling with their original experiments. The teacher had to go to the rescue of one group. Other groups were helped by 'eavesdroppers'. Eventually most finished by the deadline set.

By this time, following the whole-class discussion of individual groups' problems, the informal contact between working groups and the work-related talk among the members of each group, the teacher could tell that everyone had become fully involved with the ideas towards which he had been leading them.

Stage 5: whole-class discussion

The following single lesson was devoted to an oral consideration of the original goal: What is the energy doing? The teacher admitted he had to feed in many clues, as this was 'beyond C S E level', but the bright pupils helped. Answers to the other goal questions were supplied by the various groups, who were forced by questioners to explain the basis of their answers.

Stage 6: final stage

The teacher instructed the groups to swop among each other to find new combinations of chemicals to mix and to *predict* the nature of the reactions. In the subsequent double period there was much argument about these predictions and this led to the teacher feeling satisfied that the original ideas he had set out to teach were now part of the pupil's working knowledge.

Thus, through extensive use of talk in small groups, in whole-class and in teacher talk and using various strategies such as 'eavesdroppers' and 'questioners', this particular science teacher has, in his 'circus' method evolved a whole range of talk techniques which could readily be applied to other subjects. The great virtue of his method seems to be that while acknowledging that talk is valuable he does not let pupils talk for the sake of talking, but carefully structures talk into a whole learning programme, so that the pupils talk in a variety of circumstances and to a variety of purposes.

Douglas Barnes has suggested that the commentary which supports action and observation is different in function from both speculative and reflective talk. He has put forward the idea that science teachers plan for a special 'talk time' in groups after practical work is finished.

Conclusion

It is hoped that this 'anthology' chapter has shown how talk can be useful in a variety of ways in English lessons and in other subjects such as metalwork, mathematics and chemistry. It is also hoped that the chapter indicates a way ahead for others who may wish to pursue a similar line of research. There are many questions which remain to be answered. For example:

i   What is the difference between the commentary which supports action and observation and speculative and reflective talk? Is talk in science, mathematics and practical subjects different from that in arts subjects?

ii   Can a way be found to use talk to enable pupils to 'ask the right questions', and thus extend their learning power by enabling them to be critical about their own work rather than merely being speculative about the implications of other people's work (plays, poetry, etc.)? The questions asked in the examples on mathematics can be seen to relate to a much wider field.

iii What practical uses of talk, demonstrated in the section on interviewing, can be made part of the school curriculum? One approach to this question may be found in BBC schools radio programmes such as *Web of Language*, a series which is 'designed to stimulate children's interest in various aspects of the English language, particularly in the ways in which language is used in communication'.

The work described here is by no means definitive; the report records our experience as teachers working on a local curriculum development project. We suggest in the Introduction that it may help other teachers to make their own discoveries: we hope that it does.

Appendices

Appendix A Tape-recording, transcription and analysis: practical suggestions

Most of the project's work was based upon the close analysis and study of tape-recordings and transcriptions of pupils' talk. Making a tape-recording, transcribing it and choosing methods of analysis pose a number of practical problems. This appendix gives guidance on these problems based on the experiences of project members.

1 Making the recording

i WHY RECORD TALK?

There is considerable value in recording talk in the classroom, whether it is between teacher and pupils or between pupils only. The main purposes can be summarized as follows:

a Recording can provide a record of conversations otherwise unheard. This allows the teacher to assess the standard of oral work, to check on the progress and behaviour of members of a group and thereby reassure himself about what took place in his absence. Although teachers can often make an intuitive assessment of a group's progress, only a tape-recording provides complete and objective evidence.

b Recording gives a status to the work. It is all too easy for pupils to devalue the place of oral work in school; by recording talk the teacher invests it with significance. In this way the tape-recorder acts as both control and motivation for the group and many pupils take considerable interest and pride in the tape itself as an end-product of their talk. It is, of course, necessary for the teacher to listen to at least part of the tape if this effect is to continue to operate. It is of little value if the teacher records and then forgets the tape – his pupils will soon realize what is happening. It is equally important that the teacher does not overstress the importance of the finished tape itself for this may encourage the pupils to restrict the range and freedom of their talk in order to produce a 'good tape'.

c Recordings can be used as a teaching aid. Using the tape as illustration the teacher can discuss a group's oral work with the pupils, suggesting where weaknesses lie and how to overcome them. In addition pupils can use the tapes to assess their own performance. This is a very useful means of developing self-critical qualities. If the talk is designed to lead on to subsequent written work, many pupils find the tape useful as a form of notebook to recall ideas and conclusions.

ii   WHOM DO YOU RECORD?

Few teachers would wish or be able to record all the groups involved in talk in their classrooms. Schools may have only one tape-recorder available and teachers would find it impossible to listen to a large number of tapes produced at every talk session. Recording, therefore, will most probably take place on a very selective basis and teachers may well choose to use the tape-recorder on only one or two occasions during a term. However, it is obviously desirable to record individual groups on more than one occasion so that comparative assessments of their progress can be made. How, therefore, does the teacher select suitable groups for tape-recording?

In each class the teacher will be able to identify 'good' and 'bad' groups and the natural temptation may be for him to record those groups which will be most likely to produce worth-while results. It is, of course, very rewarding to record the most able and responsive groups; they will be enthusiastic and ready to listen to advice and guidance. However, pupils who may be less motivated in other types of work, may show considerable ability and enthusiasm in the use of talk and can demonstrate quite striking progress. It is very difficult to predict accurately which groups will be 'good' or 'bad' in oral work and teachers should beware of pre-judging pupils on the basis of their performance in other areas of their work. Many teachers may find that recordings of groups who do find difficulties in using talk will be very instructive in evolving and developing teaching strategies.

It may be possible for the teacher to select for recording purposes an 'average' group which he feels is representative of the whole class. This will probably be easiest if he selects the members of groups rather than using self-selected friendship groups.

The decision as to whether small or large groups or both should be recorded must be made by the teacher but there is value in both, as Chapter IV seeks to demonstrate.

iii   WHERE DO YOU RECORD?

There are three main areas in which recordings are likely to be made:

a   *In the classroom.* It is quite possible to record one or more groups in the same room. With suitable seating arrangements and small, portable tape-recorders the noise level need not be so great as to interfere with individual recordings.

b *Out of the classroom.* There are many advantages in dispersing groups into cloakrooms, corridors, annexes, nearby classrooms or any other rooms or spaces which are available. Groups may well appreciate the privacy offered and superior recordings can be made without the background noise of a crowded classroom.

c *Field recording.* In some situations it may be interesting and valuable for recordings to be made outside of class times and outside school itself. Interviewing, which is illustrated in Chapter V, is an example of this work. In this situation a robust, high-quality recorder with a shoulder strap and a hand-held, remote-control microphone is an advantage.

iv   HOW DO YOU RECORD?

Even the simplest tape-recorder is expensive and teachers may well find that the least expensive models may not be robust enough to take the hard use that pupils will provide. For the purposes of recording and transcribing pupils' talk there is little doubt that a cassette machine is superior in terms of convenience, cost and ease of use to an open-reel recorder. There is, of course, a bewildering choice of different makes but it is recommended that the following factors are borne in mind when selecting a machine:

a It is usually best to have a built-in microphone. These are easily forgotten by pupils and, being omni-directional, are most likely to provide audible recordings of all the group. Hand-held microphones tend to give an artificial formality to talk as pupils will only talk when holding the microphone as it is passed around the group.

b An automatic level control ensures consistent results and is proof against under- or over-recorded tapes.

c Recorders which can be run from both batteries and mains are essential. Cassette machines use a lot of very expensive batteries and most schools are well-equipped with power points.

d If you are going to transcribe tapes or use them as a teaching aid it is useful to have an instant rewind switch (no need to switch to stop every time you replay a passage), a pause control and a digital tape counter for easy identification of a passage, though none of these is essential.

e Many children have their own tape-recorder, and so are used to the sound of their own voices. Nevertheless, there are some who have not heard themselves and others who still feel that they do not sound right on a tape-recording. The way to get over this is to encourage children to use the tape-recorder themselves to listen to and monitor what they have said, and to give them the opportunity to erase part or all of a tape-recording if they do not like it. Whatever is done, it is important that the machine not be used to 'spy' on conversations where pupils do not know of its presence or are forbidden to touch it. In any case, if they have not used a tape-recorder before in the classroom, children are likely to want to go through an initial stage in which they experiment with sounds: this is natural, and should be discouraged only if it goes on for too long. The second stage consists of self-conscious utterances and performances for the tape-recorder. Eventually, however, children will not be inhibited by the presence of the tape-recorder, seeing it as a tool of work like a book or a writing instrument.

2 Examining the recording

i LISTENING TO THE TAPE

Once a recording has been made, there is no immediate necessity to do any more than listen to it. Just listening to tapes of pupils' talk can be very instructive, for there is a world of difference between hearing snatches of talk in the classroom and listening to a whole tape at home. Often, walking around the class, the teacher may hear remarks which appear to be totally irrelevant to the subject in hand and his natural reaction may be to intervene in a group's work. Yet it is quite often the case that this talk is indeed pertinent or a direct offshoot from the subject the group is discussing, as many of the examples in this book demonstrate. If the talk as a whole is listened to, the relevance of the parts is easily seen. Only by listening to pupils' talk can the complex learning processes which often take place be identified.

ii TRANSCRIBING: BENEFITS OF THE PROCESS

Although the primary benefit from recording talk is the ability simply to listen to it, transcription of sections of the recording offers additional benefits which are very valuable:

a Transcribing is a time-consuming business – about an hour is required to transcribe five minutes of talk – and thus it is necessary, when faced with a long tape, to select the most interesting and revealing sections for transcribing. This process forces the listener to assess the whole talk very carefully and, in doing so, he gains far more from his work.

b When transcribing, it is necessary to listen very carefully to everything that is said. There are many interesting features in even the shortest of talk sessions and the act of transcription itself helps to bring out these important points.

c Writing out speech often reveals aspects not noticed when the tape is just listened to. Conversely, having a transcript available makes subsequent listening to the tape an easier and more revealing process.

iii PROBLEMS OF TRANSCRIBING

The first time that one attempts to make a transcript it may seem like the most arduous task ever devised. After some practice the process does become easier and we would recommend the following procedure, although individuals will discover methods that suit them best:

a Run the recorder from the mains if possible.

b Work in a separate room from others or use headphones.

c Locate the correct place on the tape and set it running.

d Listen to the first utterance.

e Write it down without attempting to punctuate it: speech does not always fall into the pattern of written sentences. Short pauses can be indicated by a solidus (/). The solidus may be used where one would normally put a comma or a full stop; it is sometimes valuable to put in question marks and exclamation marks. Longer pauses and hesitations can be indicated by ellipses (three dots). Obvious ends of sentences before a change of speaker may be indicated by full stops.

f Leave space for words not understood or indistinct; they often become clear later in context. Write non-verbal content (e.g. laughter) in brackets and indicate pauses (timed where necessary) and passages where utterances occur simultaneously.

g If one is fitted to the machine, the instant rewind (REVIEW) key will be useful as it is usually necessary to hear an utterance a number of times to understand it correctly and transfer it to paper. If no such button is fitted, take the tape in very short sections and make use of the pause control.

h Do not attempt to identify speakers at this stage; merely place each new utterance on a new line, numbering it at the time, or later. Identification of pupils can take place later and they can often do this job themselves.

iv CONSIDERING THE TRANSCRIPT

Once you have successfully transcribed a part of the tape you have to decide what you are going to do with it. There are two basic courses open: a talk about the transcript with other interested parties (pupils, teachers, researchers, etc.); b add written comments, either alone or with the help of others. In either case, do not discard the tape; non-verbal pointers (change of voice tone, length of pause, etc.) cannot be accurately reproduced on paper and may be vital in really understanding what is going on in the talk.

a Spoken consideration of transcripts: a group of people considering a transcript of a session of talk have the same advantages as the pupils – they have the opportunity to feed on each other's intuitions and ideas and so expand their perceptions of what is going on in that talk. The value of discussing a transcript lies in the opportunity to develop ideas rather than to fix opinions. During the course of the project it became apparent that talking about transcribed talk is an extremely profitable and stimulating exercise – hours of highly charged conversation have been sparked off by relatively brief passages of talk.

b It is not always possible to work with a group of like-minded people, and some people work best within a tight framework. In these cases using a written commentary, aimed at understanding the processes at work in the talk, may prove to be valuable. The degree of structure required will vary from person to person, and there are numerous ways to annotate a transcript.

v TYPES OF TRANSCRIPT COMMENTARY

Although, as mentioned above, there are many ways to annotate a transcript, none of which is right for everybody, it may be of value to illustrate three main types:

a *General interpretative commentary following a section of transcript*
This is the briefest, though not necessarily the easiest, method of adding comments. It necessitates drawing out from the talk the themes and ideas going through it, and commenting in general terms. Utterances are numbered on the transcript in order to make it relatively easy to refer to them.

b *Single parallel comment on individual utterances*
Here a comment is made on each utterance, showing its place in the overall structure of that section of talk. This form of commentary may

also include some measure of interpretative comment at appropriate intervals.

c *Double parallel commentary: utterance plus content and interaction frames*
This is based on the model devised by Douglas Barnes and Frankie Todd.* As with **b** it is set out in columns, with a comment being made on each individual utterance opposite to it. In this case, though, the comments are divided into two 'frames' – content: how an utterance relates to the subject of the talk, and its contribution to the subject; and interaction, where the utterance is related to the social structure of the group and seen as a part of the social interaction which is always present in discussion. In order that the three methods of providing commentary, varying greatly as they do in length and complexity, may be more easily appreciated, there follows a short passage of transcript, annotated in each of the three ways.

In the following transcript, taken from midway through a discussion on UFOs, Paul was arguing that UFOs exist because he has seen one, and Jim was supporting him saying that he also knew that UFOs exist. (A further extract from this tape-recording appears in Chapter I, pp. 26–7.)

a *General interpretative commentary following a section of transcript*

1 JIM They're/about a couple of inches high/'cos if they go round in little cricket balls like Paul says . . .
2 PAUL I didn't say that.
3 CHARLES (*To Jim*) He said large cricket balls.
4 NEVILLE You said cricket balls.
5 CHARLES You said . . .
6 PAUL All right then/I said/I said/it could be a million foot wide big cricket ball.
7 JIM Yeah but/a cricket ball/you don't get a million foot wide big cricket ball.
8 PAUL I didn't say that/it was a couple of miles away/so I don't know how big it was.
9 NEVILLE No.
10 CHARLES You can't tell how big they are.
11 PAUL When I looked at it/right.
12 JIM For all you know there might be a little UFO down there/it's so small.

* See *Communication and Learning in Small Groups* (Routledge & Kegan Paul, 1977), chapter 4.

13 NEVILLE No there isn't.

14 PAUL When I looked at it/OK/I could say it was about/I'd say it was about ten miles away.

15 JIM You squashed it.

16 PAUL I said it was about ten miles away/right/and it was this size when I was looking at it/right/from ten miles away/so that's pretty good/must be pretty good.

17 CHARLES Right/so that's that.

In this extract Paul was being forced to defend and expand upon an anecdote of his about having seen a UFO. Most of the discussion was concerned with the size of the UFO. Charles seemed to be very quizzical of Paul's claims, while Jim was attempting to help Paul, firstly by referring back to one of Paul's earlier remarks (since he got it wrong he was not a lot of help here) and then by jokingly introducing the idea of relative size, attempting to ridicule the opposition (as in [15]). Paul's main problem was explaining his image of the UFO being like a cricket ball in a way that no one could misinterpret. Certainly the presence of an aggressive audience forced Paul to attempt to develop and articulate his ideas clearly.

b *Single parallel comment on individual utterances*

1 JIM They're/about a couple of inches high/'cos if they go round in little cricket balls like Paul says . . . — Jim, having been asked about the size of spacemen, incorrectly uses Paul's story to work it out.

2 PAUL I didn't say that. — Paul objects to this.

3 CHARLES (*To Jim*) He said large cricket balls. — Charles here refers back to the original story, supporting Paul.

4 NEVILLE You said cricket balls. — Neville's memory supports Jim against Paul.

5 CHARLES You said . . .

6 PAUL All right then/I said/I said/it could be a million foot wide big cricket ball. — Paul, under fire, tries to explain how he meant his original comparison to be taken.

7 JIM Yeah but/a cricket ball/you don't get a million foot wide big cricket ball. — Jim, not fully understanding, queries what Paul has just said.

8 PAUL I didn't say that/it was a couple of miles away/so I don't know how big it was. — Paul has, yet again, to expand on his original idea, this time bringing in the idea of distance.

9 NEVILLE No. — Supporting Paul.

10 CHARLES You can't tell how big they are. — Also supporting Paul.

11 PAUL When I looked at it/right.	Paul goes back to the story to explain further, but is interrupted.
12 JIM For all you know there might be a little UFO down there/it's so small.	Jim takes up the idea of size, and jokes about the possibility of a UFO being in the room.
13 NEVILLE No there isn't.	Neville denies the idea.
14 PAUL When I looked at it/OK/I could say it was about/I'd say it was about ten miles away.	Paul goes on from where he left off in [11], explaining more about distance from him.
15 JIM You squashed it.	Jim jokes about the fantasy of the tiny UFO.
16 PAUL I said it was about ten miles away/right/and it was this size when I was looking at it/right/from ten miles away/so that's pretty good/must be pretty good.	Paul presses on with his explanation of distance and the size an object seems to be.
17 CHARLES Right/so that's that.	Charles accepts this explanation.

c *Double parallel comment: utterance with content and interaction frames*
This type of transcript commentary is shown in Table a, pp. 130–1.

From these examples it will be clear that the amount of commentary increases dramatically between the general interpretative comment and the double parallel comment, single parallel comment lying between. In some ways the double parallel is the most comprehensive but also the simplest, working as it does from single utterances, and dividing comments into compartments. The general interpretative comment, on the other hand, requires an overview of a considerable section of talk at one time, and this can be more taxing.

It is, then, a question of identifying the use to which the commentary will be put, and choosing the form of annotation which best suits that purpose. As a group we used each type of commentary and found them all interesting, but the parallel commentary rather time-consuming.

Table a Double parallel comment: utterance with content and interaction frames

	Utterance	Content frame	Interaction frame
1	JIM They're about a couple of inches high/ 'cos if they go round in little cricket balls like Paul says . . .	Answers earlier question and re- fers back to earlier statement by Paul.	Accepts question . . . and passes it back to Paul by raising voice at 'cos.
2	PAUL I didn't say that.	Denies that that is what he said.	Takes up challenge from earlier part of interchange.
3	CHARLES (*To Jim*) He said large cricket balls.	Refers back to original statement.	Supports Paul.
4	NEVILLE You said cricket balls.	Refers back to original statement.	Challenge to [2] and [3].
5	CHARLES You said . . .	Refers back to original statement.	Supportive of [4].
6	PAUL All right then/I said/I said/it could be a million foot wide big cricket ball.	Qualifies statement and offers in- formation on relative size.	Accepts challenge and responds to it positively.
7	JIM Yeah but/a cricket ball/you don't get a million foot wide big cricket ball.	Misinterprets Paul's reference to relative sizes.	Takes up challenge from [1], [2] and [3].
8	PAUL I didn't say that/it was a couple of million feet wide how big it was	Denies he said the UFO was one million feet wide. Refers question	Accepts challenge and extends field of inquiry.

	...en big they are.	Accepts Paul's statement.	Supportive.
11	PAUL When I looked at it/right.	Refers back to own experience.	Continues to accept challenge.
12	JIM For all you know there might be a little UFO down there/it's so small.	Takes up fantasy offered by idea of size. Imagines minute UFO in room.	Self-assertion by joking remark.
13	NEVILLE No there isn't.	Takes up fantasy to deny it.	Challenge to [12].
14	PAUL When I looked at it/OK/I could say it was about/I'd say it was about ten miles away.	Extends own frame from [11] by continuing account of own experience.	Competes with Jim for the dominant role by effectively ignoring him.
15	JIM You squashed it.	Reacts to denial of [13] by continuing fantasy frame.	Continues competing with Paul for dominance.
16	PAUL I said it was about ten miles away/right/and it was this size when I was looking at it/right/from ten miles away/so that's pretty good/must be pretty good.	Continues question of uncertainty about size, referring to all previous remarks and to some made earlier in the discussion.	Still trying to hold his own against Jim's shared laughter with Neville. Congratulates himself – ego boost.
17	CHARLES Right/so that's that.	Continues conduct of task by suggesting that the question has been answered.	Tries to gain dominance; bid fails.

Appendix B Conclusions and recommendations on talking and listening from *A Language for Life* [The Bullock Report].

The following list of conclusions and recommendations on talking and listening is taken from *A Language for Life* (HMSO, 1975), Part 10, 'Summary of Conclusions and Recommendations', pp. 526–7.

Talking and listening

1 Exploratory talk by the pupils has an important function in the process of learning.

2 A child's accent should be accepted and attempts should not be made to suppress it. The aim should be to provide him with awareness and flexibility.

3 Children should be helped to as wide as possible a range of language uses so that they can speak appropriately in different situations and use standard forms when they are needed.

4 The teacher's own speech is a crucial factor in developing that of his pupils.

5 A stimulating classroom environment will not necessarily of itself develop the children's ability to use language as an instrument for learning. The teacher has a vital part to play and his role should be one of planned intervention.

6 Oral work should take place in both large- and small-group situations, with an emphasis on the latter.

7 Pupils should learn to regard discussion as an opportunity to investigate and illuminate a subject, not to advance inflexible points of view.

8 There should be a conscious policy on the part of the teacher to improve the children's listening ability. This is best achieved not through formal exercises but by structuring opportunities within the normal work of the classroom.

9 Efforts to develop ability in talking and listening should be supported by audio-visual resources on a proper scale.

10 External examinations in oral language are of value where they minimize artificiality and help the process of developing ability in a wide variety of uses. There should be further research into the kinds of examination best fitted to achieve this.

11 As part of their professional knowledge teachers should have:

an explicit understanding of the processes at work in classroom discourse;

the ability to appraise their pupils' spoken language and to plan the means of extending it.

There should be more opportunities for teachers to study these and other aspects of language in development work and in-service education.

12 There should be further research into the development of children's spoken language and the best means of promoting it.

Appendix C Further reading and classroom resources

Basic reference books

BARNES, D., *From Communication to Curriculum*. Penguin Books, 1976.
BARNES, D., BRITTON, J. and ROSEN, H. *Language, the Learner and the School*. Penguin Books, 1969; rev. edn, 1971.
BARNES, D. and TODD, F. *Communication and Learning in Small Groups*. Routledge & Kegan Paul, 1977.
BRITTON, J. N. *Language and Learning*. Allen Lane, Penguin Press, 1970.
Department of Education and Science. *A Language for Life*: Report of Committee of Inquiry appointed by Secretary of State for Education and Science under chairmanship of Sir Alan Bullock [The Bullock Report]. HMSO, 1975.

Books relevant to the subject of talk

CASHAN, A. and GRUGEON, E. (eds) *Language in Education: a Source Book*. Routledge & Kegan Paul, 1972.
Language in the Classroom (prepared by Douglas Barnes for Open University Language and Learning Course Team). Open University Press, Milton Keynes, 1973.
Language and Literature (prepared by David and Elizabeth Grugeon for Open University Language and Learning Course Team). Open University Press, Milton Keynes, 1973.
MALLETT, M. and NEWSOME, B. *Talking, Writing and Learning 8–13* (Schools Council Working Paper 59). Evans/Methuen Educational, 1977.
MARTIN, N., WILLIAMS, P., WILDING, J., HEMMINGS, S. and MEDWAY, P. *Understanding Children Talking*. Penguin Books, 1976.
SELF, D. *Talk: a Practical Guide to Oral Work in the Secondary School*. Ward Lock Educational, 1976.
WALKER, R. and ADELMAN, C. *A Guide to Classroom Observation*. Methuen, 1975.
WILKINSON, A. *The Foundation of Language: Talking and Reading in Young Children*. Oxford University Press, 1971.
WILKINSON, A. *Language and Education*. Oxford University Press, 1975.
WILKINSON, A. and HAMMOND, G. *Language for Learning*. Exeter University School of Education, 1977.

Classroom resources: books referred to in the text

ASIMOV, ISAAC. *The Best of Isaac Asimov*, ed. Angus Wells. Sidgwick & Jackson, 1973

BARSTOW, STAN. *A Kind of Loving*. Michael Joseph, 1964; Penguin Books, 1972.

GEORGE, JEAN. *My Side of the Mountain*. Bodley Head, 1962.

HUGHES, TED. *Wodwo*. Faber, 1967.

LUNZER, E. and GARDNER, K. (eds) *The Effective Use of Reading*. Heinemann Educational, 1979.

MCGOUGH, ROGER. 'Let Me Die a Youngman's Death', in *Penguin Modern Poets 10: the Mersey Sound*. Penguin Books, 1967.

MCLEOD, J. and ANDERSON, J. *Gapadol Reading Comprehension Test*. Heinemann Educational, 1973.

PATTEN, BRIAN. 'Party Piece', in *Penguin Modern Poets 10: the Mersey Sound*. Penguin Books, 1967.

ROSS, ALAN. 'Survivors', in *Open Sea*. London Magazine Editions, 1975.

SMITH, STEVIE. 'Not Waving but Drowning', in *The Collected Poems of Stevie Smith*. Allen Lane, Penguin Press, 1975.

STEINBECK, JOHN. *Of Mice and Men* (New Windmill Series). Heinemann Educational, 1965.

The Pearl (New Windmill Series). Heinemann Educational, 1954.

TESKY, T. H. and PARKER, F. J. (eds) *The Urge to Mate* (Themes to Explore Series). Blackie, 1972.

WELLS, H. G. *The War of the Worlds*. Heinemann, 1898; Penguin Books, 1971.

WESKER, ARNOLD. *Chips with Everything*. Cape, 1962; Blackie (Students' Drama Series), 1967.

YEATS, W. B. *The Collected Poems of W. B. Yeats*. Macmillan, 1950.

Project team, consultative committee and others involved

Project team

Geoffrey Eggins (*Director*)	Head of English Department, Nailsea Comprehensive School, Bristol
Tony Barry	Head of English Department, Worle Comprehensive School, Weston-super-Mare
Jon Pratt	Deputy Head of English Department, Worle Comprehensive School, Weston-super-Mare
Ian Graves	English teacher, Churchill Comprehensive School, Bristol
Derek Adams	English teacher, Wyvern Comprehensive School, Weston-super-Mare
Paul Balaam	Head of English Department, Clevedon Comprehensive School, Clevedon
Sally Mermoz	English teacher, Broadoak Comprehensive School, Weston-super-Mare
Nicholas Parsons	English teacher, Backwell Comprehensive School, Bristol
Heather Lyons (*Evaluator*)	Senior Lecturer in Language in Education, Bulmershe College of Higher Education, Reading
Valerie Clout (*Project Secretary*)	Secretary, Weston Teachers' Centre

Consultative committee

Jon Pratt (*Chairman*)	Deputy Head of English Department, Worle Comprehensive School, Weston-super-Mare
Ian Graves	English teacher, Churchill Comprehensive School, Bristol
Del Goddard	Acting Warden, Rachel McMillan Teachers' Centre, London; Schools Council Steering Committee B

Gerald Lawrence	Head of English Department, Newport High School, Gwent; Schools Council English Committee
Arthur Knott	Warden, Weston Teachers' Centre
Winifred Hickson (until August 1976)	Senior Adviser for English and Drama, Avon Education Authority
Iain Ball (from September 1976)	Senior Adviser for English and Drama, Avon Education Authority
Jasmine Denyer	Schools Council Curriculum Officer
F. S. Sparrow	Schools Council Research Officer

Consultants

Harold Rosen (until December 1975)	Professor of Language and Literature, University of London Institute of Education
Douglas Barnes (from May 1975)	Senior Lecturer in Education, University of Leeds Institute of Education
Frankie Todd	Lecturer in Psychology, School of Humanities and Contemporary Studies, Leeds Polytechnic

The co-operation and assistance of the following staff in schools in the County of Avon is gratefully acknowledged:

Denys John, Trevor White, Malcolm Hanson, Michael Nicholson	Nailsea Comprehensive School
Howell Griffiths, David Howe, Pat Hill-Cottingham	Backwell Comprehensive School
Michael Hinton, Margaret Ramsden, Mary Ticehurst, Gerald Moore, Pat Korovilas	Broadoak Comprehensive School
Donald Foster, Penny Blackie	Churchill Comprehensive School
William Boddy, David Hamblen, Maurice Cotton, David Pearce	Clevedon Comprehensive School
Elizabeth Ballinger, Elizabeth Cryer	Gordano Comprehensive School
Donald Brown	Worle Comprehensive School
Francis Mohan, Wyn Charles	Wyvern Comprehensive School

The following people are also thanked: Sheila Pitt and Noel Hetherington (Weston Teachers' Centre); Judy Keiner (Senior Lecturer in Language in Education, Bulmershe College); Jill Jones, Pam Payne and Ronald Searle (student teachers, Bulmershe College); Heather Walker, Wynel

Rees, Nadine Vokins, Carol Stevenson, Hazel Dean and Carol Luke who transcribed the tapes; and John Isaacs and June Braithwaite (Schools Council Field Officers).

The original idea for a language development project grew from a proposal made in 1972 by Sue Moth, now Senior Mistress at Berkely Vale School, and formerly of Nailsea School.